CHRISTIAN ETHICS
Issues and Insights

About the Author

Rev. Dr. M. Stephen teaches Theology and Ethics at Faith Theological Seminary, Mankala, Adoor, Kerala. He obtained his B.A. and M.A. degrees from Kerala University, B.D. and M. Th. degrees from Serampore University, Kolkata and his doctoral degree from Dharmaram Vidyakshetra in, Bangalore.

Dr. Stephen has several books to his credit, including *A Liberated Vision: A New Mission Agenda; Introducing Christian Ethics : A Christian Theology in Indian Context; Human Rights and Ethics of Love in Human Context.*

CHRISTIAN ETHICS
Issues and Insights

Rev. Dr. M. Stephen

CONCEPT PUBLISHING COMPANY, NEW DELHI-110059

Cataloging in Publication Data—DK
Courtesy: D.K. Agencies (P) Ltd. <docinfo@dkagencies.com>

Stephen, M. (Muthunayakom), 1959-
Christian ethics : issues and insights / M. Stephen.
p. cm.
Includes bibliographical references (p.)
Includes index.
ISBN 8180693635

1. Christian ethics. I. Title.

DDC 241 22

ISBN 81-8069-363-5

First Published 2007

Published and Printed by

Ashok Kumar Mittal
Concept Publishing Company
A/15-16, Commercial Block, Mohan Garden
New Delhi-110059 (India)

Phones: 25351460, 25351794
Fax: 091-11-25357103
E-mail: publishing@conceptpub.com

Preface

Christian Ethics: Issues and Insights is mainly dealing with the methodological issues. The theories of ethics, the modes of ethical discourses, Bible and ethics, ethics and the subalterns, Bio-ethics, war and peace, absolute and relative, Gospel's ethics, and normative and evaluative are the main issues discussed in this book.

The task of ethics is to guide the persons and communities to act responsibly in the context. God has created us to be human and responsible as He is, and this is very evident in the life of Jesus. He guided the persons through his fitting or responsible words and deeds. The aim of ethics is to lead the people to do what is good, right and responsible so that the welfare of all or the liberation will be made possible.

I hope this book will help the readers and especially the students of ethics to develop a humane and responsible approach so that they may be a channel of blessing for others.

Rev. Dr. M. Stephen
M.A., M.Th. Ph.D.
Puthenparambil
Near Railway Station
Kottayam-686001
Kerala

Contents

1

Definition and Development of Ethics

The word 'ethics' comes from the Greek word 'ethos' which means customs or behaviour. The adjectival form in Greek is 'ethica'. The word morality comes from the Latin word 'mos' which also means character or behaviour of life. The adjectival form is 'mores'. Morality is more concerned of the personal moral behaviour, but ethics regards the foundational aspects as very significant and it deals with the structural elements also.

According to Richard Niebuhr, ethics as an intellectual enterprise enables us to bring more clarity into our interpretation of the social world—analysis of values, goals and aspirations (*Responsible self*). He continued to say that ethics helps us to understand ourselves as responsible beings and exercise it in our community. It is through the action of persons that it affect the social world.

Ethics is the systematic study of the nature of value concepts. What actions are right, wrong, good or evil? At different times and circumstances man's behaviour can be varied. In advanced countries there are various types of social norms, e.g., legal, religious, moral and conventional. The variations are due to the difference in moral import of the "same" acts in different social situations and institutionalised frameworks.

Socrates has suggested three arguments: (1) We ought never to harm anyone, (2) We should obey the laws of the state, (3) One's society or state is virtually one's parents and teacher, and one ought to obey one's parents and teachers (*William Frankena, Ethics,* p. 2). According to Frankena, "ethics is a branch of philosophy, it is moral philosophy or philosophical thinking about morality, moral problems and moral judgements" (*Ethics*, p.14). In the opinion of Frankena we can distinguish three kinds of thinking that relate to morality:

1. There is a descriptive empirical enquiry, historical or scientific, such as is done by anthropologists, historians, psychologists and sociologists. Here the goal is to describe or to explain the phenomena of morality or to work out a theory of human nature which bears on ethical questions.
2. There is a normative thinking of the sort that Socrates was doing in the Crito or that anyone does who asks what is right, good or obligatory. This may take the form of asserting a normative judgement like "I ought not to try to escape from prison", 'knowledge is good' or 'It is always wrong to harm someone'.
3. There is also 'analytical', 'critical' or meta-ethical thinking. It does not try to answer either particular or general questions about what is good, right or obligatory. It asks and tries to answer logical, epistemological or semantical questions like the following: What is the meaning of use of the expressions "(morally) right" or "good"? What is the nature of morality? What is the meaning of 'free' or 'responsible'? (*Ibid.*, pp.4-5)

Morality is understood a social enterprise. It is not just a discovery or invention of the individual for his own guidance. Morality is sometimes defined as an instrument of society as a whole, as if an individual, family, or social class cannot have moral action guide of its own that is different from that of its society. Morality also has a individualistic aspect. As Socrates implied and recent philosophers have stressed, morality fosters or even calls for the use of reason and for a kind of autonomy on the part of the individual, asking him, when mature and normal, to make him own decisions. Even as a social institution of life, morality is thought of as aiming at rational self-guidance or self-determination in its members. There is a difference between pre-rational, customary or group morality and personal, rational or reflective morality (*Ibid.,* p. 7).

There is pre-Socratic and post-Socratic Ethics. Kant made ethics an integral part of philosophy. The ethics of Plato can't be treated as a finished product but rather a continuous movement from the position of Socrates towards the more fully articulated system of Aristotle. The first development from the Socratic position carried the problems from morals into metaphysics. Socrates had initiated a search for definitions. Heraclitus said that the world around us is always in a state of flux and change. Socrates said 'virtue is knowledge'. Plato said truth, goodness, reality and value, philosophy and morals are related to one form, the form of the good. Ethics, according to Diogenes, is concerned with the foundation of human behaviour. Aristotle, Plato, Kant, Hegel, Marx and even other ancient and modern philosophers and ethicists have conceived ethics in different ways. To Aristotle, ethics is a branch of politics. This is because, ethics is the science of the good and politics is the science of the highest or supreme good.

There are different types of ethics: Deontological, teleological, and contextual ethics. They can be defined as the principle-oriented, goal-oriented, responsibility-oriented or context-oriented ethics. For James Gustafson, ethics is a contextualist response of situations. Contextualists, as against the deontologists, are for what is 'fitting' rather than the universal norm. J.A.T. Robinson says that there is a tension between the constant and the variable, the absolute and the relative, the eternal and the changing. In the changing socio-political and economic condition, ethics and ethical problems need to be viewed in a new perspective, says D.R. Bali. The ethics of Hinduism, Islam, Christianity and other religions are undergoing considerable change in the modern world. The modern challenges and issues are totally different from the ancient so also the decisions. The concept of love is understood in a new way amidst the new ethical challenges. The personal problems became unimportant and the structural problems held dominance. The socio-economic exploitation, injustice and political bondage are seriously considered. The role of liberation ethics is important here. The situation ethics of Fletcher and responsibility ethics of Richard Niebuhr and other contextual ethics became eye-openers to the traditional principle oriented ethics. The natural law tradition is also questioned. The changes or variations are arising from changes to knowledge or belief regarding the quality of acts and their consequence. There is an aspect of evolution and revolution in the realm of morality or ethics.

Aristotle argues that the ethics should aim at what is good. The good is happiness for him. He urges us to choose the fine, the beneficial and the pleasant, and to avoid the shameful, the harmful and the painful. In his book '*Ethics*', Aristotle states that the supreme good is happiness. In the understanding of idealism, the mind and spiritual values are more fundamental than material ones. It is opposed to naturalism which explains the mind and spiritual values in terms of material things and process. Hegel was an idealist. In Hegelian view spirit alone is reality and all reality is the outworking of the spirit (*Philosophy and Christian Faith* by Colin Brown).

Ethics is understood as the science of customs or habits. It is the science of the habitual conduct of men. Ethics evaluates the voluntary and habitual actions of persons and considers their rightness and wrongness (*A Manual of Ethics*, by Jadunath Sinha, p.1). Ethics provides guidelines for ethical judgement and it does have normative and evaluative dimensions. Ethics imparts a vision that the persons and communities are to uphold. It *foresees* an attitudinal and perspectival change and radical transformation. It is praxis oriented and liberating. Ethics also discerns what is going on in the society and urges us to respond in a fitting manner in the context. Ethics reflects on issues and inspires us to creatively respond to the issues.

The following are the definitions for ethics given by different scholars. According to James Gustafson, Christian ethics is the intellectual discipline that draws normative inference from the experience of the reality of God for the conduct of the Christian community and its members. In his view, Christian Ethics is contextualist response to situation (Can Ethics be Christian, p.179).

For Paul Ramsey, basic Christian Ethics must itself always theory oriented towards practice. His ethical approach is based on agape that is inprincipled love. The obedience to God and covenant—love are significant in his ethical perception. Christian Ethics is deontological in nature in his view (*Basic Christian Ethics*, p. XI).

Dietrich Bonhoeffer states that the knowledge of good and evil seems to be the aim of all ethical reflection. Ethics is understood as formation—Christ formation. It is the bold endeavour to speak about the way in which the form of Christ take form in our world (*Ethics*, p. 3).

M.M. Thomas states that the Christian obligation is to be defined as criticism and transformation of the moral sense present in a situation in the light of ultimate ethics of love and fellowship. The goal of Christian Ethics is the immediate realization of as much agape and koinonia as possible in the present and re-orientation of the direction of life to its full realization in the future (*Christianity*, p. 52).

K.C. Abraham defines that Christian ethics as a discipline should provide guidance for action and criteria for judgement and discernment. This evolves out of involvement in concrete situations (*Bangalore Theological Forum,* Vol.XVI, 1984, p. 61).

In the perspective of Hunter P. Mabry, while moral conduct may be used to refer to actual behaviours, Christian Ethics is best understood in terms of critical reflection upon such things as assumptions, explanations, consequences and justification offered for specific activity which have a moral dimension (*Christian Ethics: An Introductory Reader*, p. 213).

Enrique Dussel has the view that Christian Ethics is the affirmation of life emerging from the experience of community, the experience of the relations of a respectful love among the sisters and brothers. For him, the Jerusalem principle stands for life, justice and sharing, and 'Babylonian Principle' represents death and oppression. He develops ethics from the Latin American context (*Ethics and Community*, p. 105).

2

Theories in Ethics

There are different theories of ethics exist. They provide different understanding.

The Deontological and Formalistic Ethics

These ethical theories are duty-oriented ethics. According to Thomas Kadankavil, "these theories stress the duty or obligation in the ethical consciousness and hold that the rightness or the wrongness of an action depends on the action itself and not on the consequences it produces" (*Ethical World*, p. 2). Kantian ethics is also deontological as duty is insisted on persons from the respect of the law. Keeping the law or universal rules is important for Kant. It is imperative, that is it ought to be obeyed. It is unconditional. The absolute rules found in natural law is also deontological in character. The Roman Catholic morality is also deontological in nature.

Act-deontological theories, especially extreme act-deontologists maintain that we can and must see or somehow decide separately in each particular situation what is the right or obligatory thing to do, without appealing to any rules and also without looking to see what will promote the greatest balance of good over evil for oneself or the world, states Frankena (*Ethics*, p. 16). In his opinion, E.F. Carrit, H.A. Pritchard, and Aristotle come close to this view. Act-deontologists insist on the particular obligations like 'in this situation I should do so and so'. "In a less extreme form, act-deontologist allows that general rules can be built upon the basis of particular cases and may then be useful in determining what should be done on later occasions", says Frankena (*Ethics*, p.17). Situation ethics is related to act-deontologism.

The rule deontologists holds that the standard of right and wrong consists, or one or more rules fairly concrete are like "we ought always to tell the truth", states Frankena. He further explains that as against the act-deontologists, they content that these rules are basic and not derived by induction from particular cases. They assert that judgements about what to do in particular cases are always to be determined in the light of these rules (*Ibid.*, p.17). According to Frankena, "people who take 'Conscience' to be our guide or standard in morality are usually either rule-deontologists or act-deontologists, depending on whether they think of conscience primarily as providing us with general rules or as making particular judgements in particular situations" (*Ibid.*, p.17). The Act-deontologists are concerned of the particular situations in their judgements and rule-deontologists insists on general rules. Samuel Clarke, Richard Price, Thomas Reid, W.D. Ross, Immanuel Kant and Paul Ramsey belong to the category of rule-deontologists.

The Teleological Ethics Aims at What is Good

Aristotle's ethical approach is teleological as it aims at good. Happiness is the perfect good for him. In hedonism also one can notice the pleasure as the aim. The good is pleasure for hedonistic philosophy. The epicurean thinking (eat, drink, be merry, tomorrow we will die) is related to it.

According to Frankena, "the so called utilitarians, for example, Jeremy Bentham and John Stuart Mill, have usually been hedonists in their view about what is good, asserting that the moral end is the greatest balance of pleasure over pain" (*Ethics*, p.16). It is noted that not all utilitarians are hedonists. G.E. Moore and Hastings Rashdall are "Ideal" utilitarians. It is a kind of teleological theory of obligations and does not entail any particular theory of value. The Act-utilitarian is concerned of the good of the society in general as rule deontologists simply appeals to rules. Rule utilitarian defends those rules on the ground that having such rules and always acting on them for the greatest general good.

Gross utilitarianism is sensualistic. It is promoted by Jeremy Bentham. He does not admit qualitative differences among pleasure.

In this view, any one pleasure is as good as another provided they are equal in quantity. A pleasure is pure when it is unmixed with pain, for Bentham (Jadunath Sinha, *A Manual of Ethics*, p.75).

Qualitative utilitarianism is ascribed to John Stuart Mill. The greatest happiness principle is asserted by hedonist J.S. Mill. For him, actions are right in proportion, as they tend to promote happiness, wrong as they tend to produce the reverse of happiness. Happiness is explained as pleasure or absence of pain. Pleasure and freedom from pain are only desirable ends. Virtue, health, and love of honour are means to happiness, for him. Mill recognizes the kinds of pleasure or the qualitative difference of pleasures—the distinction of quality. For him, some kinds of pleasure are more desirable and valuable than others.

Rational Utilitarianism is ascribed to Henry Sidgwick. He promoted intuitional or rational utilitarianism. In his view, pleasure is the only intrinsic value. It is good in itself. It is the reasonable or rational object of desire. He identifies conscience with practical reason, pleasure is ultimately desirable (*A Manual of Ethics*, p. 102).

Ideal utilitarianism is related to H. Rashdall. He founded his utilitarianism on reason as Sidgwick. The moral faculty for Rashdall is reason. He considers it as moral reason or practical reason, which intuitively apprehends the highest good. Highest good are virtue, knowledge, beauty and happiness. Values or moral judgements decide what is good. For him, right is the means to the good. An action can be right only if it is conducive to the universal wellbeing or happiness. Rightness of action depends on its consequences and if the result of the action is subversive to the universal wellbeing, it is wrong. Rashdall's utilitarianism is classified as 'ideal' as it aims at the maximum good in the individual life irrespective of the different moments. It also regards others' good as of equal worth as our own good. He understands justice on not equal distribution, but as equitable distribution.

G.E. Moore also came under the category of ideal utilitarianism. He holds the intuitive notion of good. For him, 'good' is indefinable. He opposes the view of the hedonists who compares good with pleasure. Good for Moore is an organic whole (*A Manual of Ethics*, p. 205).

The Act-utilitarianism is concerned of the good that every decision brings over evil in each situation. Telling the truth is good guide, but the question is whether telling the truth will bring greatest general good in the particular case. Situation ethics is act-utilitarian. (Frankena, *Ethics*, pp. 35-36).

General utilitarianism holds that if something is right for one person to do in a particular situation, then it is also right for anyone else who is similarly situated to do, and therefore that one cannot ask simply what effects one's proposed action will have in a particular case—one must ask what the consequence would be if everyone were to act likewise in such cases (*Frankena, Ethics*, p. 38). For general utilitarian, if an action is right for him to do in his situation, then it is right for everyone to do who is similarly situated.

Rule-utilitarianism is attributed to J.S. Mill. It emphasizes the centrality of rules in morality. It asks the question which rules will promote the greatest general good for everyone. The question is not which *action* has greatest utility, but which *rule* has (Frankena, *Ethics*, p. 39).

The Ethical Egoism is Based on the Following Tenets

That an individual's one and only basic obligation is to promote for himself the greatest possible balance of good over evil. That even in making second and third person judgements, an individual should go by what is to his own advantage. Ethical egoists are hedonists and they identify good or welfare with happiness. These are the observations of William K. Frankena (*Ethics*, p.18).

Absolute and relative ethics: According to Thomas Kadankavil, "The former holds that it is possible to have a universal and eternal moral code which is not subject to changing circumstances. The relativistic ethics holds that the moral standard varies with different circumstances (*Ethical World*, p. 3).

The objective and subjective ethics: According to Kadankavil, "this division depends on whether 'good' or 'right' are taken to be objective, standing for a real factor in things or subjective, simply standing for a human proposal. All forms of absolute ethics are necessarily objective ethics. Subjectivist ethics is a form of relative ethics which holds that the circumstances which cause variability in the moral judgement is a mental state of a particular person" (*Ethical World*, p. 3).

Naturalistic and Non-naturalistic (Intuitionist) Ethics

The former holds that 'good' and 'right' can be known as natural objects are known and that their empirical verification is possible in ethics. The latter holds that the right and good can be known only by a special intuition and so they are also known as ethical intuitionists. These both theories are cognitive theories (*Ethical World*, p. 3).

Non-cognitive (Emotive) Ethics

According to non-cognitive theory, ethical terms do not stand for anything objective. They do not assert moral facts. There is nothing to be known by 'moral intuition'. Ethical terms and judgement stand for emotions, attitudes, proposals, recommendations etc. It is the emotive theory. It grounds ethical terms in emotions expressing the attitude of approval or disapproval (*Ethical World*, p. 3).

Divine Command Theory

It is also known as theological voluntarism: It holds that the standard of right and wrong is the will or law of God. An action is made right or wrong ultimately is its being commanded or forbidden by God. The right and wrong is decided on the basis of whether God commanded or forbidden it.

3

Modes of Ethical Discourses: Deontological or Contextual

In the ethical reflection, there are different patterns of ethical discourses developed.

Deontological Ethics

The Roman Catholic morality is based on the natural law which emphasize the dictate of the practical reason. The natural law insists on certain orders in the society. Thomas Aquinas was influenced by Aristotle who rely on the natural law. Charles Curran brings to our attention the ambiguity of natural law. He states, "natural law in the broad sense of the term refers to the humanity and reason which all men share in common. Natural law in the more restricted sense refers to a particular understanding of humanity based on nature as a principle of operation in every living thing including human beings" (*Ongoing Revision in Moral Theology*, p. 31). The traditional Roman Catholic understanding is rooted in natural law. Curran again writes that according to their view, the creator has imprinted an order in the universe which live in the hearts of men. In the nature of man and the universe, conscience can find the order and norms by which men are guided together to live in peace and harmony. Roman catholic morality based on natural law is legalistic and not considering seriously the experience and crisis of the persons. It is based on do's and don'ts. The abortion, sterilization and use of contraceptives are always wrong according to Roman Catholic morality. It is quite *a priori* and absolutistic in nature.

The legalistic interpretation of the law in the Bible is also related to this problem. Law is reduced to be inhuman and legalistic by the

Pharisees in Jesus' time. They rejected the law of love and approved the love of the law. This is what Jesus questioned and taught them about the love which is the essence of the law. The loveless rules were rejected by Jesus. The laws related to Sabbath was inhuman and unloving which were not approved by Jesus. Legalism is quite found in natural law, Roman Catholic morality and in the Judaistic and other rigid interpretations of the law. They are merely rule oriented and based on abstract principles.

The 'Dharma' in the Indian context is also very deontological in nature. It stands for duty. The personal duty (*Svadharma*) and caste duty (*kuladharma*) are very significant in this respect. There is also a division of *sadharana dharma* (ordinary duty) and '*Sanatana Dharma*' (duties which are eternal and universal in nature). The problem with *dharma* is that it is very much based on caste duty. By birth, everyone is dutiful according to his caste. *Brahmin* is to involve in religious duties. *Kshatrya* is to wage war regardless of his particular interest. *Vaisya* is to do business. The *Sudra* is to do mean jobs. These are all duties for duties sake and very legalistic. There is no mobility for the so called lower castes. It is also very exploitative or oppressive. These rigid and inflexible laws are inhuman.

Emmanuel Kant is famous for his *a priori* rules. His ethics is intuitive and deontological in character. It is based on duty for duty sake. Kantian ethics insists on promise keeping and telling the truth always. He proposes the categorical imperative by which it is imperative to tell the truth whatever might be the situation. The *a posteriori* dimension is disregarded by Kant. He emphasized the role of reason and the dictate of the conscience in his ethical approach. Morality is understood by him as 'practical reason' as he believed that the exercise of reason is very important in man's sense of right and wrong. Duty is an essential factor of practical reason. Universal law of reason and universal law of morality are one and the same in his perspective. The categorical moral imperative is enforced by the universal law. He does not approve any exceptions in rule. The ethics is made more unconditional and abstract by Kant. It is rooted in natural law. The 'ought' is significant in Kantian ethical approach. In contrast to the categorical imperative, Kant introduces the hypothetical moral imperative, which is more related to issues like health and hygiene. It is conditional and it is not binding. It is good, if an individual take care of the health and hygiene rules and concerns. It is relative according to the necessity and situation. For him doing duty is an imperative regardless of the consequences. Kantian ethics is also very legalistic and not concrete. The rules are important but rules for the sake of rules or duty for the sake of duty is not adequate.

Paul Ramsey, the American ethicist is a staunch advocate of deontological ethics. His ethical approach is influenced by the natural law and conventional wisdom. The deontological ethics is for universally valid rules. 'Agape' or love is his norm, but it is rooted on rules or principles. The covenant-love or obedient-love play a dominant role in his ethics. His approach is rule—agapism. It is the inprincipled love or *a priori*—agapeic approach. His main books are "Basic Christian Ethics' and 'Deeds and Rules in Christian Ethics'. According to Ramsey, the concept of love is essential for any moral action and the two sources of Christian love, for him, are God's righteousness and the reign of the righteousness in the Kingdom of God (*Basic Christian Ethics*, p. 2). Love as embodies in Jesus Christ plays a decisive role in his ethical thought. According to Ramsey, God's love in alignment with God's gracious acts has the power to direct attention to the requirements of faithfulness and to make these as 'canons of loyalty' primary in the moral life and our system (*Deeds and Rules in Christian Ethics*, p. 91). Ramsey permits exceptions very hardly. Extra-marital sex is infidelity for him, but he allows the pre-ceremonial sex of the engaged couples on the ground that they become married thereby. Abortion is condoned only in the case of the child becomes a villain. His argument for the pre-ceremonial sex among engaged couples is not suiting to his approach and cannot be approved by the Christian normative approach. Ramsey's approach is criticized as legalistic as it is not considering the context seriously.

Teleological Ethics

The teleological approaches are significant modes in ethics. It is aim or goal oriented ethics. What is good is the main question asked in teleology. The main question in deontology is "what is right"? In the situation ethics and new morality the main question is what is loving? The Kingdom of God, liberation, happiness and pleasure can be understood by different people as the aim. Better tomorrow is the common wish of all men and communist ideology looks forward the classless society or dictatorship of the proletariat. A world that transcends exploitation, indignity and injustice is their aim. They work for a socialistic society.

In Aristotle's thinking also there is teleological dimension. The telos of his ethical approach is happiness. The supreme aim for him is ultimate happiness. In the hedonistic philosophy, pleasure is the goal. This is very much reflected in the perspective of Epicurus who said, "eat, drink and be merry; tomorrow we will die". Happiness and pleasure are good for both Aristotle and hedonism. In the common cultural understanding also good is pleasure, welfare, or prosperity. A better tomorrow is the aim. The hope plays a very significant role in our daily life.

In the Christian view, the eschatology is deep rooted in hope. The Kingdom of God is the aim. It is the new community. It is a new structure. It is an egalitarian society. Kingdom of God is having two dimensions. The realized eschatology stressed the tension between 'already' and 'not yet'. The 'future' is also related to the present. Jesus said that Kingdom of God is in our midst as he inaugurated the Kingdom. The first sphere or dimension is in process, and there would be a final realization.

Kingdom of God is the central category for Wolfhart Pannenberg. For him, future is the beneficent, future is the father who cares, it is the father who is love. Love, according to him, is the force of coherence therefore the future is not in radical discontinuity with the past and present but promising fulfilment to past and present (*Theology and the Kingdom of God*, p. 27). His eschatological understanding relates past and the present.

Past and present are inextricably interwoven. In Pannenberg's view, the quest for good, seeking what is good for human beings, still provides the best starting point for ethical investigation. For him, God is the ultimate good not in isolated transcendency but in the future of the Kingdom. He further states that the striving for God as the ultimate good beyond the world is turned into concern for the world (*Ibid*., p. 111). He also opined that the future of the Kingdom releases a dynamic power in the present that again and again kindles the vision of man and gives meaning to his fervent quest for the political forms of justice and love. He argues that the Kingdom of God guards the freedom of individuals and will enable the individual to commit himself to society.

Jurgen Moltmann's hope theology also concentrates on the Kingdom of God. In his view, proper theology has to be constructed in the light of its future goal. Eschatology should not be its end, but its beginning (*Theology of Hope*, p. 164). Future is, for him, the continuation of the regular recurrence of the present. In his view, hope's statements promise to anticipate the future. They lead the existing reality towards the promised and hoped for transformation (*Ibid*., p.17). Hope, in his view, keeps man unreconciled until the great day of the fulfilment of all promises of God. He states again that this hope makes the Christian a constant disturbance in human society as it works towards righteousness and freedom (*Ibid*., p. 20). In Moltmann's view hope and resurrection are linked as he believes that Christian hope is directed towards a new creation of all things by God of the resurrection of Jesus. He tried to reconcile hope and praxis.

Both Pannenberg and Moltmann are concentrating on hope and the Kingdom of God which are teleological in character. But their teleology is not merely futuristic, but a teleology which closely links the future and the present.

Carl Braaten does discuss the ethics in relation to eschatology and Kingdom of God in his book *Eschatology and Ethics*. His ethics also has a teleological thrust. According to him, traditionally eschatology is understood as the 'last things', but in modern times (*e.g.* Albert Schweitzer) eschatology is brought back to the centre of Christian thinking. For Braaten, the eschatological future of the Kingdom of God is real. In his view, it is Pannenberg who understands the significance of eschatology for doing Christian Ethics. Braaten realizes that eschatology provides the bridge between the past and present. Christian Ethics announces, anticipates and approximates the Kingdom. Kingdom of God is the ultimate goal for teleological ethics, states Braaten.

Walter Rauschenbusch developed a theology for the social Gospel. He also uses the Kingdom of God as the Key category. He was looking forward the social transformation. Kingdom of God, for him, is terrestrial or this worldly. He was working for organizing the society in the light of the concept of the Kingdom of God. The aim is the structural change and for him salvation is not individual, but collective as sin is not merely individual but collective. Kingdom of God is not transcendent, but a progressive movement of the society for Rauschenbusch. He was for christianisation of the social order. He had the hope in the coming of the Kingdom of God as a historical possibility.

New Morality and Situation Ethics

There is a tension between constant and variable, absolute and relative, eternal and the changing according to John A.T. Robinson. He argues that the old morality is based on fixity, law and authority, but the new morality is founded on freedom love and experience. (*Christian Morals Today*, p. 7ff). The three polarities will well describe the nature of the 'old' and the 'new' morality. He charges that old morality clings on what is absolute (there are certain things which are always wrong) or eternally valid in the midst of relativity and flux (*Ibid.*, p. 11). In his view, the laws of God or the commandments of Christ is to be applied to the changing situation. The new morality asserts that "Bible supplies a God given 'net' or framework of conduct for human affairs. The task of the moral theologian is to keep the net in repair for each generation and to define its mesh more closely as new occasions teach new duties" (*ibid.*, p. 12). He feels that love has superiority over law.

The problem with J.A.T. Robinson is that his new morality is very relative as it supports the abortion and the pre-marital sex, though his ethics upholds the responsible freedom and love. As a normative the abortion, premarital sex or extra-marital sex cannot be justified. But these can be forgiven in a situation where a person looks for love and mercy. Here the evaluative dimension can be applied as a remedy to resolve the problem with love and humanness.

The situation ethics is proposed by Joseph Fletcher. As a reaction to the legalists, Fletcher has said that they cry for doing 'right' even if the heaven falls (*Situation Ethics*, p. 13). Fletcher's situationism is based on love and not on *a priori* rules. For him, a decision in an existential moment or situation is important. He states that the only absolute of new morality is agapeic or loving neighbour concern, and it seeks the good of the people by decisions tailored to the relativities of each particular situation [Joseph Fletcher, "Why new?", *Religion in Life;* Vol. XXXV No. 2 (*Spring* 1966), p.188]. A decision in a situation is authentic Kairos for Fletcher. As we found in Robinson, the love is the norm of Fletcher also. 'Only one thing is intrinsically good; namely love; nothing else at all'. Love only justifies the 'means', 'love and justice are the same', 'love is the only norm', 'love only decides then and there' are his main prepositions. In the context of abortion, euthanasia, extra-marital sex, pre-marital sex and artificial insemination, he raises very crucial questions which need very serious attention though law brings good to an extent, it can reduce to inhuman. The ethical approach of Fletcher is *a posteriori* agapeic in nature as it deals with the context of the victimized. From the Christian perspective his approach cannot be normative, but evaluative only. Though one cannot accept the irresponsible sex, abortions, pre-marital sex or euthanasia, there are cases where persons look for guidance in their crises. In the case of Mrs. Bergeimer, she looks for mercy where it should be granted though extra-marital sex is evil. She took a decision to have 'extramarital sex', to save herself in an 'extraordinary' situation. She should be granted mercy, from the evaluative perspective. Fletcher's argument for normative to legitimate evil cannot be accepted as his approach is only evaluative from the Christian view.

Contextual Ethics

A radical shift has been taken place in ethics as ethics has become contextual. The contextual ethics gives utmost importance to the context or the experiences of the people. The socio-political realities are also considered seriously. It is an ethics from below as against the ethics from above. It is not a dictated ethics as we found in the deontological ethics. It is not prescriptive or principle oriented but it is rooted on agape. It is sensitive to the issues and the love, and humanness play a crucial role in the ethical decisions. It is a paradigm shift in ethical methodology.

The chief proponent of contextual ethics is Paul Lehmann. His famous book is *'Ethics in a Christian Context'*. He was talking about ethics in the industrialized and dehumanised western society. The context of Christian community and the context of the world are important for him. Two questions are important for Paul Lehmann. What God has done and is doing in the world? and What am I to do? The answer to the first question is, God is *keeping human life human*, according to Lehmann. The answer to the second question is, Our responsibility is to involve actively in the humanizing activity of God.

Lehmann's Ethics is Koinonia Ethics, as Koinonia manifests a new fellowship between Jesus Christ and the faithful. He argues that "A Koinonia ethic claims that such human relationships are actualised in the world in consequence of and in the context of the concrete reality of the church" (*Ethics in a Christian Context,* p. 131). According to him, "In the Koinonia a continuing experiment is going on in the concrete reality and possibility of man's interrelatedness and openness for man" (*Ibid.*, p.131). Koinonia Ethics is concerned of concrete situation and the issues related to it.

Lehmann was quite aware of relevance and significance of contextual ethics. He states, "the primary ethical reality is the human factor, the human indicative, in every situation involving the interrelationships and the decisions of men. In the Koinonia something is already going on, namely, what God is doing in the situation out of which the ethical question and concern arise to fashion circumstances and behaviour according to his will? This is why a contextual ethic does not lead to ethical anarchy or ethical expediency" (*Ibid*., p. 131). The Koinonia Ethics is concrete and relational. Koinonia ethics or contextual ethics do consider the context and the community seriously, and it is not personalistic. What is 'human', is very significant for Paul Lehmann's ethical approach.

Lehmann discusses also the theonomous conscience by which one is sensitive to God's freedom and his activity. God sensitivized conscience is understood as significant for realizing what God is doing in the world. For him, Christian ethics aim at maturity and the new humanity. In his view, an absolutistic ethics cannot deal with the real ethical command. The transfiguration of politics (messianism) play a crucial role in Lehmann's ethics. He looks for structural transformation.

The 'Responsibility-Relationality ethics' of Richard Niebuhr is found mainly in his book the '*Responsible Self*.' In his book '*Christ and Culture*', he argues that Christ transforms the culture. As against deontological and Teleological ethics, Richard Niebuhr suggests 'responsibility'. He was influenced by existentialism and the 'I and Thou' concept of Martin Buber. According to Richard Niebuhr, the great God has created us as responsible beings. Responsibility inquires, he said, what is going on? What is fitting action or response? *Man the maker* is able to reject what is not suiting to his purpose. It is teleological in nature. Teleology is only concerned of what is good. It rejects what is not suiting to good. *Man the citizen* represents the deontological ethics. It is bound by duty and living under the dictate of law. The third symbol is *man the Answerer*—the man engaged in dialogue. Man acting in response to action upon him is implicit in the idea of responsibility. In the ethics of responsibility, the fitting action, the one that fits into a total interaction as response and as anticipation of further response conducive to good and is right. According to richard Niebuhr, 'Responsibility affirms—God acting in all actions upon you so respond to all actions upon you as to respond to his action'. There are four elements in the theory of responsibility. They are as follows:

1. The first element is *idea of response*. All moral action is response to action upon us.
2. The second element is *interpretation*. It is not only responsive action. But response in accordance with our 'interpretation' of the question to which answer is being given, 'what shall I do?'
3. *Accountability*. It is the anticipation of reaction to our reaction. Our actions are made in anticipation of answers to our answers. Responsibility lies in the agent who stays with his action who accepts the consequence in the form of reaction and looks forward in a present deed to the continued action.
4. *Social solidarity*. Our action is responsible when it is response to action upon us in a continuing discourse or interaction among human beings forming a continuing society.

The fitting response is the key factor in Responsibility-Relationality ethics. As a social being we are to respond to the things that happen. According to Richard Niebuhr, the responsive or responsible self is not a machine. The question of freedom, he states, arises in this connection as the question of the self's ability —in its present to change its past and future and to achieve or receive a new understanding of its ultimate historical context. He understands the Christian life in terms of responsibility as he realizes that Christ was having a responsible dutiful life. Deontology looks for what is right? teleology concentrates on what is good? but responsibility stresses the fitting action.

The responsibility ethics is also found in Dietrich Bonhoeffer. In his book 'Ethics' Bonhoeffer explains the responsibility. According to him, structure of responsible life is conditioned by two factors: life bound to man and to God and man's own life is free. Without this bound and freedom, there is no responsibility. He further express the view that responsibility is fundamentally a matter of deputyship is demonstrated most clearly in those circumstances in which a man is directly obliged to act in the place of the other men, for example, as Father and as statesman. No man, he states, altogether escape responsibility, *i.e.* no man can avoid deputyship. In his view, we have to be responsible to ourselves, and to others and also to the mankind. In his opinion, Jesus made clear his deputyship to mankind as performing the responsibility.

According to Bonhoeffer, only selfless man lives responsibly. Deputyship is responsibility, in his perspective, and it lies in the complete surrender of one's own life to the other man. It is relational, as responsibility, as life and action in deputyship, is essentially a relation of man to man. He argues that the responsible man is dependent on the man who is concretely his neighbour in his concrete reality. Responsibility is understood by him as a vocation and is related to obedience. He states that responsibility is the total realistic response of man to the claim of God and of our neighbour.

Responsibility ethics is also upheld in Bernard Haering. It is explained in his book *The Law of Christ.* The mark of response is very significant for a truly religious ethics, in his view. Man is to respond to God's word in the responsibility of his personal decision and action. He is much influenced by the natural law as he is a Roman Catholic Ethicist, but at the same time he takes the concrete reality seriously. The correct response, he says, precisely to the extent that man takes his terrestrial tasks seriously and earnestly accepts created values. In his understanding, to be a member in the Kingdom of Christ demand of us the responsibility of active participation.

The theological ethics of James Gustafson is theocentric in nature. It has also a teleological and contextual thrust. God and good are the central theme of his ethical approach. Locus of good is God and God is the determiner of good and the source of the ultimate good (*Christ and Moral Life*, pp. 26-27). According to him, Christ frees us from legalism, and Christ is the norm for Christians. His criticism against deontological ethics is that it does not take seriously the perplexity and ambiguity of all human existence. He also argues that the situational or contextual ethics expose the complexity and predicament of the human condition and consequently our decision and action, but made the discernment of the good too relativistic, subjective and individualistic. According to him, if Christian life is directed towards a goal, it is a goal determined by a vision of God's goodness. He states that Christ provides the clue to the goodness.

The basic question in Gustafson's ethical approach is, what God is enabling and requiring us to be and to do? God is enabling men to discern what God is enabling men to do; but the locus for the discernment is in the self as it relates belief about the God in whom it trusts to the situation in which it acts. A certain amount of contextuality is found over here. In his opinion, "Christian Ethics will be more likely to guide persons to the right action than more intuitive approaches will' (*Theology and Ethics*, Vol.1, p. 69). The main aim of his ethics is to bring good and to glorify God. For Gustafson Christian ethics is a contextualist response to situation. There is a contextual dimension in Gustafson's ethical approach.

In James Gustafson's perspective, men are called to respond to what God in his grace is doing for them; they are accountable to him for the life they live in the response. He, further, states that an understanding of moral responsibility is crucial for the participation of the Christian community in the moral life we share with all men (*Responsibility in Modern Religious Ethics* by Albert R. Johnson, Washington, Corpus Books, 1968, pp. VIII-IX).

According to Albert R. Johnson, God has created man to be free and responsible. Denial of political responsibility is said to be denial of God's intention of man and his work of salvation. He talks about responsibility in terms of personal, social and political. In his words, responsibility apparently describes an attitude or quality of character which those created and called to responsibility should possess (*Ibid.*, p.17).

The major influence of responsibility ethics is Karl Barth's understanding of God, the actor. God is acting, and man is to act upon what God is acting? According to him God cannot draw man to himself without involving him in responsibility. He continues to say that live in responsibility means our being and willing, what we do and what we do not do, is a continuous answer to the word of God spoken to us as a command.

The responsibility ethics is inspiring us to be responsible. God is a responsible being. As a responsible being he responds to a human situation as he humanizes and liberates. Jesus' incarnation was the embodiment of God's responsibility. God is active in history as he responds. God's love and redemption are indicting his responsibility. So human beings are indebted to be responsible to the fellow human beings as their creator.

Charles Curran is a contextual ethicist. He questioned the natural law and the legalistic ethics. He was not happy with the Roman Catholic morality and challenged its inadequacy in the changing context. One of his famous book was entitled, 'Ongoing Revision in Moral Theology.' According to him, Christian should be open to what is human in the situation of science and human experience. The norm of Christian conduct for Curran is the demand of love in the concrete situation. He realizes the importance of the shift from classicist methodology to a historically conscience methodology. While the classicist methodology emphasizes what is eternal, universal and unchanging, the historically conscious methodology gives more attention to the historical, the contingent, the personal and the existential.

Middle axioms is another important contextual dimension in ethics. According to Russell Chandran, John C. Bennett's perspective of ethics is a re-statement of J.H. Oldham's middle axiom. Bennett's concerns in ethics is twofold, first, to find a rational basis for applying the Christian faith and secondly, to state moral judgement in such a way as to promote moral co-operation and dialogue with people of other faiths. He interpreted middle axiom as being more concrete than a universal ethical principle and less specific than a programme that includes legislation and policy. Dr. Chandran views Bennett's middle axiom as very helpful for concrete decision-making. He further states that when the ultimate goal is beyond our reach and the universal ethical principles do not provide guidelines for immediate action, middle axioms challenge us to seek penultimate goals which are realizable (*Christian Ethics*, p. 94).

Liberation Ethics

Gastavo Gutierrez is known as the father of liberation theology. His famous book is *A theology of Liberation*. The liberation theology was emerging from Latin America, where there was colonialism and oppression and extreme poverty. In this context, the oppressed and poor sought their liberation. They saw the dynamic and liberating God in Bible. God is having solidarity with the poor. God has a preferential option for the poor.

Gutierrez argues for the commitment to God and neighbour. The 'orthopraxis' or rightness in acting is given importance by him. For him, communion with the Lord means a Christian life centred around a concrete commitment of service to others. In his view, a theology that linked to praxis fulfils a prophetic function. According to him, Christ is presented in the Bible as the one who brings us liberation. Liberation express the aspirations of the oppressed. The exodus and second exodus are political actions, for him. He sees a methodological shift in liberation ethics, perceiving the truth to doing the truth. According to Gutierrez, "when justice does not exist, God is not known, he is absent" (*A Theology of Liberation*, p. 195).

Jose Miguez Bonino in his book '*Towards a Christian Political Ethics*' has made the following reflections. According to him, political ethics is an indispensable instrument for the struggle. He states that in the Latin American context, we found it necessary to relate our theology to a commitment to the struggle for liberation, a struggle that has pre-dominantly social and political dimension. In his view, incarnation becomes the clue for the understanding all of God's dealing with human history and with reality. An incarnational ethics would affirm:

1. The ultimacy of the christological determination of ethical priorities, whereby Jesus Christ in his historical and permanent ministry is the measure and the power of God's purpose in the world.
2. The significance of historical action and fulfilment as assured in God's permanent concern, initiative, and act for humanization in history.

In Bonino's view, God is the redeemer, the liberator and the avenger of the oppressed.

Enrique Dussell has the liberative expression in his book *'Ethics and Community'*. According to him, Acts of the Apostles (2:42-47) recalls for us that the essence of the Christian life is community : being together with others. This is also the reign of God: to be together with God, face to face with God in community. In his view, praxis denotes any human act addressed to another human person and praxis is both act and relationship. The system of sin is taken seriously by his ethics of liberation. He also talks about the 'Babylonian principle' and the 'Jerusalem principle'. The Babylonian principle is the order of oppression and the Jerusalem principle is the order of Koinonia and the new community. Liberation ethics, in his opinion, affirms human dignity and freedom.

The liberative aspect is found in M.M. Thomas, Sebastian Kappen, and K.C. Abraham in the Indian context. M.M. Thomas talks about the rights of the poor and their mobilizing for liberation. Jesus is found by him as the source and foundation of humanization. He visualizes the social or structural transformation. He proposes a prophetic spirituality or spirituality of combat to question the unjust and oppressive structures which hinders the liberation. According to him, revolution is to humanize and to create human dignity. He was for the socio-political justice and trying to relate religious commitment to social commitment. His ethics is contextual, 'human' and liberative.

Sebastian Kappen could find a liberative spirit in *Bhakti* tradition, Jainism and Buddhism. According to him, Jesus can be a sure clue to an authentic existence and a source of inspiration in the struggle for a new humanity. He looked for a non-exploitative and egalitarian society. According to him, Christ provides freedom and challenge for organized struggles. Kappen's ethical perspective is praxis-oriented and it challenges the dehumanising structures. For him, theology and ethics have to be sensitive to the cry of the poor and oppressed (*Liberation Theology and Marxism*, p. 5ff).

The ethical perspective of K.C. Abraham is more concerned of the poor and the oppressed. It is an ethics of the marginalized.

His key concern is the liberation of the oppressed. He gave importance to justice, freedom and dignity. His ethics is committed to the victimized women, dalits and tribals and the poor. His ethics is a life affirming ethics and his approach is contextual, praxis-oriented and liberative.

The issues of the black and other subaltern groups are very significant in Christian ethics. The blacks raise very crucial questions in relation to their dignity, freedom and liberation. They are taken to North America and elsewhere as slaves. In South Africa they were colonized by the whites. In North America, Martin Luther King Junior played remarkable role in the civil rights movement to liberate them from the clutches of the discrimination by whites. In South Africa, under the dynamic leadership of African National Congress leader Nelson Mandela they had been liberated.

The Black ethics is an ethics of liberation. It is an ethics which inspires the blacks to work for their identity, dignity and liberation. This ethical approach challenges the systemic evil, the apartheid (colour prejudice) and the oppression and look for the liberation of the blacks. It is contextual and liberative ethics. It is an ethics which is praxis-oriented. The exodus event is understood by them as the impetus to their hope, says James cone, the black theologian. God is understood as the liberator of the blacks. The black ideology recognizes the poor as the central focus of the Gospel. The sin is found by it in the exploitation by the rich and the hatred of the neighbours.

The liberative ethics is found in the Minjung theology which insists on the aspiration, hope and the liberation of the Minjung of Korea. The same is found in the women theology and ethics which questioned the patriarchy and other dehumanising elements. They also look for gender justice and liberation as against the misogynist attitude and the domestic and societal oppressions. The women argue for their dignity and equality. The women liberation movements are for social and political freedom and active participation of women. The feminist ethics is for the liberation of women. In the tribal theology and ethics also the aspect of liberation is found. They also challenge the violence and the exploitation.

They are for their integrity, autonomy and freedom. The strong spirit of liberation is found in the *dalit* theology and ethics. The questions of the *dalits* are very crucial over here. It is a centuries long oppression which is based on caste. It is social, economic, religious and political in nature.

The *dalit* ethics is rooted in Triune God as liberator. He liberates the people of Israel from the bondage, so also the *dalits* will be liberated by God from the Brahminic and other dominance. Gospel is for the liberation of the subaltern or *dalits*. The Nazareth manifesto is the *dalit* manifesto. It is God's plan of liberating the *dalits* or the crushed ones. The *dalit* ethics questions the exploitation and oppression of the dalits. Their social, economic and political freedom are a very important concern of *dalit* ethics. It is a praxis oriented ethics.

The liberation ethics is a praxis-oriented, contextual and liberative ethics. It is a communitarian ethics. It is an ethics with social and political commitment. It is a ethics which struggles for life against death. In the liberation theology and ethics the Marxian analytical tools are used critically. It also integrates the prophetic spirituality and Jesus' approach of liberation. The incarnation, cross and resurrection play important roles in the understanding of liberation.

The contextual ethics and liberation ethics are ethics from below and they are concrete rather than abstract. As against the deontological and teleological ethics, the contextual and liberating ethics are quite related to the ground realities. So they can be called as 'Bullock-cart Ethics' (An ethical version of S.J. Samartha's 'Bullock-cart Theology'). There is room for love, humanness and justice in the contextual and liberation ethics. They are more experiential and political. The issues are taken seriously and discussed in detail before coming to a conclusion in contextual and liberation ethics. The situation ethics is also relevant to an extent, but it should be only approved as evaluative than normative. The poor are of great concern in the contextual and liberation ethics. They are liberating or humanizing. The 'right' of the deontology and its legalism and the 'good' of the teleology only have a limited scope to be responsible in ethical decision-making.

4

Absolute, Relative and Relational in Ethics

There is a tension between absolute and relative in ethics. This is true with Christian ethics also. The undue importance given to rules lead to absolutistic ethics. The absolute principles used to stand above the reality. Absolute is very exclusive and it is against the inclusivism. Absolute claims can be only applied to God and nothing to do with the other realities as it stands for 'nothing beyond'. All realities cannot be interpreted in terms of what is absolute. There are views such as God as absolute, love as absolute and freedom as absolute. For Jean Paul Sartre, "freedom is the only source of value and of the nothingness for which the world exists". Heraclitus, the Greek philosopher realizes the reality as relative. He perceives the relativity and flux of the context. Ernst Troeltsch talks about the historical relativism, the ongoing changes in history is stressed.

The absolutistic is abstract and is understood to be unrelated to the concrete reality. The question is whether any rule or action is always right? Is telling the truth always right? Those who supports deontological method are also providing room for certain exception. Paul Ramsey holds that pre-marital sex is evil, but he permits the pre-marital sex of the engaged couples, which is an example for this. There is absolute nature found in ethics, but also the relative aspects. The extreme absolutism is dangerous. The absolutism has to be examined and determined in the light of the context. Love can be absolute, but it cannot be exclusive, abstract and fixed or unmoving. It has to be related to the analytical observations and issues of the context.

Relativism is a fact. Ethical relativism is the contribution of the diversity of cultures and social setting. According to Paul Tillich, the various cultures and religions have contributed to ethical relativism (*Morality and Beyond*, p. 20ff). Each culture and religion has their own rules, principles or code of behaviour. For example, among the tribal culture and in Islam, polygamy is common, but in secularised and Christian context, the monogamy is insisted. It is not easy to absolutize or universalise these ethical codes as they are confining or relevant to the particular situation. The catholic moral theology is based on natural law which insists on the absolute rules or norms. The 'old' or traditional morality is against relativism. J.A.T. Robinson states in the '*Honest to God*' that the 'old' (morality) thinks that 'new' (morality) is belonging to what is wrong and might be selling out to relativism. He also talks about the tension between absolute and relative.

Paul Lehmann the contextual ethicist explains that an 'absolute' is a standard of conduct which can be and must be applied to all people in all situations in exactly the same way. There can be general rules or principles, which are meant for the whole humanity, but the fact is that all the rules cannot be applied to all the contexts in the same way. It is also true that in certain situation all these absolutes can be applied, but not in all situations as the issues and the contexts are different. The absolutes are also *a priori* in nature so they do not apply to what is *a posteriori*. It is good to say 'keep the promises', 'tell the truth always' or 'do not commit adultery', but when one has violated these absolutes and in crisis, a relative and relational approach is necessary to help the persons. The moral absolutes (categorical imperative) in Immanuel Kant are based on don't 'break the promises' and 'don't tell lies'. It also asserts doing the duty is the obligation irrespective of the consequence'. His ethics is more intuitive and *a priori* and not related to the context. In the natural law ethics also the 'reason' and the 'absolutes' are highly regarded. The order and harmony are supposed to be created on the basis of universal laws. It is also not concrete, but abstract.

The 'Responsibility' and 'Relationality' are very crucial in ethics. Ethics is to be relational. It should be related to the context. God related himself to history and humanity as a responsible being. Jesus was also relating to the world in a very creative way through his incarnation. Richard Niebuhr's ethical approach is also a relational one. The contextual ethics are relational ethics, as they are related to the people, community and context. For Richard Niebuhr, the self is always in relationship to others and is governed by these relations. Man is related to God and to the fellow human beings and their context so there should be relatedness or relationality in the dealing of man and in his ethical decisions.

Martin Buber develops the proper relationship in his 'I-Thou' paradigm. His book is also entitled 'I - Thou'. He is for a dialogical relationship. He rejects subject-object or 'I-It' relationship. I-Thou is a relationship of openness and mutuality and it is a creative relationship. This relationship can be between man and man, and man and God, the Eternal Thou. Life is dialogical and relational so also ethics should be concerned of the dialogue and relationality. The relationality dimension provides ample room for perceiving the reality and to make suiting decisions on the issues.

5

Ethics and the Use of Bible

The Bible is the source for Christian ethics. Bible provides the ethical perspectives as it has the ethical vision or insights. The Biblical interpretation plays a pivotal role in Christian ethics. The proof-text method is an erroneous method so also the peripheral attempts like the spiritualization. Rudolf Bultmann suggests content-exegesis, i.e., what is said and what is meant. He is for demythologization. Paul Tillich suggests the deritualization. A deconstruction is necessary for the realization of the meaning of the text. A deconstruction of iconoclasm is inevitable in order to have the adequate meaning of the text. This process is also found in the literary and Rhetorical interpretation. The '*Dhvani*' (resonance) interpretation of India is quite related to these hermeneutical principles. The language and its structure and implication are very significant in this respect. The symbols are integral to language and each symbol has a variety of shades of meaning.

What is important is the 'meaning' in hermeneutics. We also today discuss the issue of the 'meaning' of 'meaning'. There is also 'surplus meaning' which interpretators are concerned about. The hermeneutics is seeking 'understanding', the perceiving of meaning is very crucial in the Biblical hermeneutics also. Evangelist Philip was asking the eunuch whether he could understand the text (*Book of Isaiah*). He said that he could not, so Philip was explaining the meaning to make him understand. In the philosophy also the main concern is understanding the reality. The 'meaning' or the 'truth' is expressed in the medium of folklore, folksongs, myths, symbols or poetry. The task is to grasp the meaning or the truth. The hermeneutic grasps the meaning, its implications and try to apply it to the present context.

The 'hermeneutics of suspicion' is proposed by Paul Ricoeur, which is widely used in the modern Biblical hermeneutics. The text carries the cultural ethos, which can be oppressive, so the text is suspected in order to redeem it from the oppressive spirit. This is much avail by the feminists. In the feminist hermeneutics, the hermeneutics of suspicion is greatly applied to save the text from the spirit of patriarchy or male chauvinism. The 'hermeneutics of suspicion' felicitate the deconstruction process, which is quite essential for the ethical vision also. Ricoeur also talks about 'surplus meaning' of the text, that the text assumes new meaning in the changing or new context.

The Marxian societal analysis is critically used in the Biblical interpretation. The sociological interpretation is also very much found in the Biblical hermeneutics. The subaltern issues are concerned of exploitation, oppression and margination. The non-liberative forces are very much centred around the capitalist forces. Marxian tools also provide clues to how the haves or burgeosie try to oppress the havenots.

Marxism foresees the classless society, a new world or the dictatorship of the proletariat or the subaltern. Marxism looks forward the emergence of the new structure by the conflict of the opposites. The historical dialectics and the synthetic view of life and society is found in Hegel. The total restructure or structural change of the society (this is what is meant by revolution) is the goal of communism. The liberation hermeneutics draw inspiration from Marxian thought to an extent. God is understood as the liberator. Bible is depicted as a book of liberation. The Kingdom of God is equated with a socialistic pattern of society or community. The thrust of the Bible for humanization or the liberation from the structural evil which are found in the form of exploitation, socio-political oppression and poverty.

In his book 'Theology and Christian Ethics', James Gustafson provides three ways by which Gospels can be related to morality.

1. Gospels can be interpreted to provide a theological justification for the moral life. It is stated that the ultimate

reason for being moral is that God has shown his love towards man, and thus man, both out of joyous gratitude and out of obligation to God, is to be concerned for the well-being of others.

2. The second way in which Gospels can be related to moral life is by interpreting them to provide moral commands, rules and principles to be applied to particular moral acts.
3. Gospels can be related to the moral life by interpreting them to influence the development of the 'sort of persons' members of the community become.

According to Gustafson, "The varieties of literature in the Gospels, the beatitudes and the commands, the parables, the narrations of the actions of Jesus, live out the manner of life that is worthy of the gospel of Christ, the bearing towards one another that arises out of life in Christ Jesus" (Hunter Mabry, *Christian Ethics: An Introductory Reader*, p. 179).

In the OT, the Decalogue (Ex.20:13ff) plays a pivotal role in the understanding of ethics. The Decalogue provides a general idea and clue to the ethical perspectives. The Decalogue is introduced as God given laws. The essence of the law is 'Love God and love your neighbour' (Dt.6:5). God is to be loved and one has to obey his will. The Commandments are the general principles by which the persons and communities are to be guided. The Decalogue or the laws are the guide to the way of life or to the 'walk of life'. Respecting others and abstaining from stealing, murder and immorality are the key factors in the Decalogue. The law is given for the organizing and the harmony of the society. It is provided for building a proper relationship and life together in the community.

Jesus did give importance to the spirit or the essence of the law than the letter of the law. In the Sermon on the Mount (Mt. Chapt. 5-7), he was re-interpreting the law based on the essence of the law. For Jesus, not only the act of adultery, but one who looks at a girl with lustful eyes also commits adultery. The thinking, the attitude and the action are closely related. The action comes from the very thought. In the perspective of the Sabbath laws also

Jesus asserts the humanness. Law should be human. It should be humanitarian and has to inspire us to love and serve others. Jesus demands the sensitivity of the law in the context, and not the rigidity. In the application of the law one should be very sensitive and loving.

The creation, covenant, the exodus, the teaching of the prophets, the incarnation and the Kingdom of God provide clues for the interpretation of the Bible for doing ethics. God's intent of redeeming or liberating the universe in a holistic way is the main thrust of these concepts. The creation consists God's liberative purpose. It is God's plan to create harmony in chaos. The 'Imago Dei' in humanity represents the equal status of all. The covenant plays crucial role in the organization of the community. It made the people of Israel united and responsible. Since they are indebted to God, they are also to be responsible to fellow human beings. The caring and sharing aspects are integral to the covenant. The covenantal law urges the concern towards the poor. An egalitarian society is foreseen so the liberative spirit is found in covenant.

The exodus is a response of God. God responded towards a people who cried for help. The exodus is a dynamic political activity which challenged the slavery (political unfreedom) and diverse kinds of oppressions. It was a movement towards life from death, and also to form a community. Exodus was a challenge to evil structures. It was a holistic liberation: the cross and resurrection of Jesus also provides clue to humanization. These are the symbols of righteousness, justice and God's love to all humanity. Our God—understanding is that he loves and liberates everyone regardless of caste, race or gender. He has a preferential option for the subaltern.

In the teaching of the prophets and the concept of Kingdom of God, the emergence of a new social order is rooted in justice, equality and love is foreseen. The challenge of evil such as exploitation, discrimination and injustices are found in them. They focus on the restoration and the transformation.

Restoration or liberation of the poor and the transformation of unjust socio-political structure was integral in the teaching of the prophets and Kingdom of God. A God /Christ centred socialism is the goal. The just relationship and just community are the focus.

In the eschatological hope, the advent of the new heaven and new earth, and also the transformation of the structure in a radical sense is found.

For the ethical reflection, Bible has to be interpreted in the light of the whole message of the Bible. The proof text method is not an adequate approach. The original context (context of the text) and the present context are to be bridged. It is introduced as the 'fusion of horizons' by Hans George Gadamer. Bible and the issues of the context should have a dynamic dialogue to develop a proper response. Our understanding of God, the Bible and the context are significant in the evolving of the ethical response.

One should be aware of the challenging, transforming and liberating motif of the Bible in order to make a fitting ethical response. The dynamic message of the Bible has to be recognized for the formation of ethical reflection. The 'deconstruction' in the understanding of the Biblical message is significance in this respect. The political reading and the re-reading are very essential. The fresh understanding of the scripture and the resultant iconoclasm are inevitable. Jesus said, 'you will know the truth and the truth will make you free'. This is true with the use of Bible in the ethical reflections in each generation. We have to be sensitive to the 'signs of the times' (Troeltsch) as we make ethical reflections, otherwise it would be irrelevant.

6

A Study of the Ethics in the Gospels: Selected Issues

This is an attempt to study the selected ethical issues such as love and law, and sex and marriage found in the Gospels.

The Background of the Gospels' Ethics

This chapter deals with two important aspects: one, the legacies of the earlier Hebrew religion which is very much related to the understanding of the Old Testament, and second, the Judaism at the time of Jesus which is sometimes known as later Judaism. According to Ernest Scott, "The two great sources on which Jesus undoubtedly draw were the Old Testament and the teachings of later Judaism" (Ernest F. Scott, *The Ethical Teaching of Jesus*, New York: The Macmillan Co., 1925, pp.14-15). It is quite certain that the teachings of the Gospels on the issue such as 'love and law' and 'sex and marriage' are quite influenced by these two elements. The influence of the Old Testament and the later Judaism is very evident in the sayings of Jesus and the formation of the Gospels.

The Influence of the Early Hebrew Religion

R.E.O. White had dealt with this subject very vividly in his book *Biblical Ethics*. (R.E.O. White, *Biblical Ethics, The Changing Continuity of Christian Ethics,* Vol. I, Exeter: The Peternoster Press, 1979, pp.13-30) (The word 'Judaism' also needs some clarification. Judaism is the religion of the Jews. It evolved out of a long history. It has so many phases. The earlier phase of it is very much associated to the Torah and the whole Old Testament itself. According to R.P. Martin, "Judaism is the religion of the Jews in contrast to the Old Testament". [R.P. Martin, "Judaism" *The New Bible Dictionary* (Reprint), edited by J.D. Douglas, England : Inter-Varsity Press, 1976, p. 670]. He regards the beginning of Judaism with the Babylonian exile (*Ibid.*, p. 670). Technically this may be quite an adequate view. Strictly speaking, the word 'Hebrew' and Hebraic religion are technically related to pre-exilic phenomenon. The term 'Jew' and Judaism are associated to exilic and post-exilic period.

The Decalogue plays a dominant role in the life of the people. According to R.E.O. White, "We have the Decalogue in two forms (Exodus 20:1-17; Deuteronomy 5:6-21) both ethical in content; a third, (Exodus 34:1-26) is concerned with ritual". (R.E.O. White, *Biblical Ethics* Vol. 1, *op.cit.*, p. 17). The book of the covenant is another significant element which helped the formation of the morality of the Old Testament people. White says, "Exodus 20:22 to 23:19 comprises a social code of *ordinances* (Precedents existing from previous priestly decisions), *warnings* and *exhortations*, making together a document described in Exodus 24:7 as the Book of the Covenant." (*Ibid.*, p. 670). According to White, the main principles of the Book of the Covenant are philanthropy, piety, justice and responsibility which is a fair summary of the whole trend of Old Testament ethics (*Ibid.*, p. 22).

White also describes the earlier prophetical teaching in this regard. He argues that "For Amos, Ethics was the basis of the covenant between Israel and Yehweh: an amoral religion God simply despises". (*Ibid.*, p. 23). Amos also, he says, rebuked the injustices and licentiousness (*Ibid.*, p. 23). Hosea hails the fidelity of God and his love. White opines that Hosea protested against the drunkenness and sexual viciousness, and he sees them as Israel's insult and affront to divine love (Hosea 2:2f). The concept of God as faithful lover is derived from God's greatest demand for *hesed* between men, for faithful love as the fount of sympathy, purity, devotion, loyalty and fidelity at all costs and in all circumstances (6:6; 10:2; 2:19, 20). (*Ibid.*, p.24).

Isaiah of Jerusalem was also against all social evils. He was for justice and condemned the sensuality and luxury (3:16; 4:1; 10:1-4; 1:10-17; 29:13-14). (*Ibid.*, p.24). Micah is portrayed by R.E.O. White as one who insisted upon the righteousness of Yahweh (2:1, 2;6:8; 3:9-12). He linked righteousness with the vindication of the oppressed (*Ibid.*, p. 24).

According to R.E.O. White, the Deuteronomists sought to incorporates the high morality of the eighth century prophets in a body of laws for civil and religious reference which insist upon justice, holiness and humanity (*Ibid.*, p. 25). He expresses the view that "In a revised edition of the book of the covenant, with new emphasis upon humanitarian morality and inward devotion to the giver of life (Deuteronomy 6 and 7), priests and prophets together presented to Josiah a programme for reform (*Ibid.*, p.25). He argues that it was to affirm God as righteous and to abolish the evil practices (*Ibid.*, p. 25).

The later prophetic tradition (Jeremiah, Isaiah 40-66, Ezekiel, Jonah, Nahum, Zephaniah, Zachariah, Malachi) also were concerned of the new covenant and emphasized the love and justice. According to R.E.O. White, Jonah developed universalism of Amos; Nahum emphasized the eternal principles of God's government; Zephaniah condemned the avarice, dishonesty and corruption, Zechariah called to a national repentance and obedience (7:1-10); Malachi was mainly concerned with religious attitudes, saw the cruelty of divorce (2:13-16; 3:1-3) (*Ibid.*, p.26), White rightly observes, "Jeremiah, Ezekiel and Isaiah 40-66 contributed major insights to the ethical inheritance into which Jesus came" (*Ibid.*, p. 26).

Jeremiah has shared the full ethical ideals of the Deuteronomists, but he lost confidence in the code of the moral requirements and in the old covenant as he looked forward to a new covenant (11:1-13; 31; 31-34) (*Ibid.*, p. 26). The old covenant has given importance to external display rather than inward change. The stress on new heart and the inner motive of the covenant is very much fulfilled in and through Jesus. According to Father Antony Edanad, "In the Old Testament it is only Jer.31:31-34 that speaks about a 'new covenant' as such" (Antony Edanad, *Christian Experience and the New Covenant*, Bangalore: Dharmaram Publications, 1987, p.7). It looked forward to future, in his opinion. Discussing on Jeremiah's perception on Israelite society, he says that their sin is presented as rebellion and is described as the exploitation, oppression (5:26-28; 6:6f; 9:5; 23:10; 34:16), and marital infidelity, which is the disruption of marriage (5:7, 8; 7:9; 9:1) (*Ibid*., p.13).

While reflecting on the new covenant and Ezekiel, father Edanad observes that Ezekiel 36:22-32 (especially vv.24-27) is thematically and even verbally very close to Jeremiah 31:31-34. And he feels that "as in the new covenant promise of Jeremiah the forgiveness of sin is the basis of the restoration and internal renewal, in Ezekiel the purification precedes the internal renewal and restoration of the covenant relation and thus serves as their basic condition." (*Ibid*., p. 13).

According to White, Ezekiel "seek refuge for her resentful pride in the dogma of collective responsibility, laying all blame upon an earlier generation. In protest he proclaimed unqualified individual responsibility (chapter 18) (R.E.O. White, *op.cit*., p. 27). He also argues that Ezekiel's thinking is more attached in this respect to Deuteronomy (18:5-9) (*Ibid*., p. 27). In his own words, "The 'righteousness' for which the individual is held responsible is defined as much as Deuteronomy would define it" (*Ibid*., p.27).

According to R.E.O. White, Isaiah (40-66) brings to harvest the ethical insights which upholds justice, love and righteousness (*Ibid*., p.28). While reflecting on the new covenant of Isaiah he said "although the covenant which Yahweh promises to make with the people is never called a 'new covenant', but, as in Ezekiel, it is specified rather 'an everlasting covenant' (Is. 54:10), the basic features of this covenant correspond to those of the 'new covenant' in Jeremiah and the parallel promises in Ezekiel" (Antony Edanad, *op.cit*., p. 55).

Regarding the holiness code (Lev. 17-26), White observes that it has a special significance to Israel since it demands humanity, philanthropy, loyalty to fellow-members, love for God and clear perception of divine holiness (R.E.O. White, *op.cit*., p. 29).

The Judaism of Jesus' Time

For Judaism, the 'Torah' plays a very important place in its theology. 'Torah' means instruction or teaching. According to Lange, "At its narrowest, it is the technical term for the most authoritative of the Sacred Scriptures, the 'Five Books of Moses' or Pentateuch" (Nicholas De Lange, *Judaism*, Oxford: Oxford University Press, 1986, p. 24). He states again that "central to rabbinic theology is the concept of the revelation at Sinai" (*Ibid*., p.27). Torah consists of commandments and regulations. Judaism is the way of life of the community. In Jesus' day the practices were different among various Jewish sects such as Sadducees, Zealots and Pharisees.

Among these groups also there are differences of opinion on the law. The Sadducees only believed in the written laws, but Pharisees respected the rules of conduct not recorded in the Mosaic laws; they called them 'tradition of the fathers'. On this feature, Lange comments, "According to one late commentary, God revealed to Moses the Whole Bible, the Talmud, the Midrash and even the answers which would be given at any future time to the questions of a student" (*Ibid*., p. 26). Commenting on this issue, Jeremias said, "The divine law of the old aeon is laid down in the Torah, or more exactly in the two *torot*, the written Torah and the oral Torah. The written Torah comprises the Pentateuch" (Joachim Jeremias, *The New Testament Theology,* Vol. 1, London: SCM Press Ltd., 1971, p. 204). He again explains that "the Torah has to be interpreted so that it can be applied to the particular instance. Thus the oral Torah arises, named Halakah. It is the work of the scribes. These has a tendency to attach the same authority to it as to the written Torah" (*Ibid*., p. 204). So it is clear that there was a written Torah and also a 'tradition of the elders' (oral law).

According to James Dunn, the interpretation of Torah took two forms—Halakah and Haggadah. In his words, "Halakah was a specific declaration of God's will in a particular case, a rule of right conduct to guide the inquirer in the way he should go" (James D.G. Dunn, *Unity and Diversity in the New Testament*, London: SCM Press Ltd., 1981, p. 62). The rulings of the teachers are passed on and preserved and are linked together which is called by Mathew as 'the tradition of the elders'. According to Dunn, it was first codified and written down in Mishnah (*Ibid.*, p. 62). The Haggadah is meant for edification and not for regulating conduct which are preserved in Midrashim (*Ibid.*, p. 63). According to Dunn, "The Pharisees might see the Halakah as part of God's Torah and delight in it—obedience to it was obedience to God" (*Ibid.*, p. 63).

R.E.O. White has the opinion that Hasidims, Pharisees and scribes saw the supremacy of law and the law dominated the later Judaism. He tells again that "the standards set by Judaism was high. Against sexual aberrations and infanticide the law was stern; if less so on divorce, it was yet more austere than among surrounding peoples" (R.E.O. White, *op.cit.*, p. 42). While dealing with the issue of 'Jewish world of Jesus' time, Fr. K. Luke opined that the Sadducees emphasized the freedom of will, teaching that man was the author of his own destiny, the Pharisees accepted the traditions of the elders or oral law and the Essences stressed the observance of continence, the purity and Sabbath [K. Luke, "Society Divided by Religion: The Jewish World of Jesus' time" In *Bible Bhashyam* Vol. 1, No.3 (September 1975), pp.197-198]. The Qumran covenanters enforced strict rules of discipline as they were for goodness, charity, love and for monogamy, and were against lust (R.E.O. White, *op.cit.*, pp. 44-45). The Rabbinic literature and non-biblical literature express the views of the time on several issues. The 'twelve patriarchs' give prominence to love for God and for the neighbour, to forgiveness, purity of heart and right intention. R.E.O. White quotes "I loved the Lord, likewise every man with all my heart" (Testament of God 6:3, of Issachar 7:6). (*Ibid.*, p.42).

The influence of the Old Testament and later Judaism is very much seen in the Gospels. According to Joachim Jeremias, Jesus has found many references of the Pentateuch as the basic norms of the will of God (e.g. Mark 7:10 par; 10:19; 12:28-34 par) (Joachim Jeremias, *New Testament Theology*, Vol. 1, *op.cit.*, p. 206), but he rejected the oral tradition or Halakah in a radical way. Especially he fought against the Rabbinic Halakah on the Sabbath (*Ibid.*, p. 28).

The Ethics of the Gospels: Selected Issues

This chapter deals with the two issues—the 'law and love' and 'sex and marriage'.

The Ethics of the Synoptic Gospels: Selected Issues

In this section, the issues such as 'law and love' and 'sex and marriage' will be taken into consideration. It is certainly from the perspective of the Synoptic Gospels. In the Synoptic Gospels, the teaching of Jesus is the dominant element, though the writers have their on prejudice and motif.

Law and Love

The law and love has a dominant place in the teaching of Jesus. Jesus' mission was for the fulfilment of the law (Mt. 5:17). According to George Eldon Ladd, "His messianic mission and the presence of the kingdom are the fulfilment of the law and prophets" (George Eldon Ladd, *A Theology of the New Testament*, Michigan; William B. Eerdmans Publishing Company, 1974, p.125). According to Joachim Jeremias, "In Mark 12:28-34 par., Jesus describes loving one's neighbour as the greatest commandment after loving God, and in Matt.7:12 he calls the golden rule the sum of the whole of the New Testament," (Joachim Jeremias, *New Testament Theology,* Vol. 1, London: SCM Press Ltd., 1971, p. 212) The six antithesis of the Sermon on the Mount (Mt. 5:21-48) have contrasted the old law and the new law. The conflict stories in Mark (2:23-3:5) and other passages related to the Sabbath also have tremendous importance in this question.

Reflecting on the six antitheses in Mathew, John Stott, the New Testament scholar, has said, "in each antithesis ('you have heard that it was said... but I say to you....') he rejected the easy going tradition of the scribes, re-affirmed the authority of Old Testament scripture and drew out the full and exacting implications of God's moral law." (John R.W. Stott, *Christian Counter-Culture: The*

Message of the Sermon on the Mount, England: Intervarsity Press 1978, p. 25).

The Pharisees gave importance to the oral law or the 'tradition of the elders' and neglected the interior disposition of the law which resulted in legalism (Rudolf Schnackenburg, *The Moral Teaching of the New Testament*, Kent: Burns & Oates, 1982, pp. 67-69). Schnackenburg argues that "Jesus knew himself to be sent by God to expound Old Testament law, in which God's will is inalienably contained, in its true sense, its ever valid claims and the obligation it imposes to act upon it, and in this way 'fulfil' it." (*Ibid*, p.59). Jesus was very much concerned with the fulfilment of the divine will. Bultmann comments, "as interpretation of the will, the demand of God, Jesus' message is a great *protest against Jewish legalism i.e.* against a form of piety which regards the will of God as expressed in the unwritten law and in the tradition which interprets it, a piety which endeavours to win God's favour by the toil of minutely fulfilling the law's stipulations" (Rudolf Bultmann, *Theology of the New Testament,* Vol. 1, London: SCM Press Ltd., 1974, p.11).

Fr. Joseph Pathrapankal as he discusses about the Sermon on the Mount also observes that "Jesus does not want to qualify anyone as his disciples observing the letter of law. He wants him to imbibe the spirit of the law and that means giving to the very basic understanding of the law" (Joseph Pathrapankal, *Christian Life: New Testament Perspectives*, Bangalore: Dharmaram Publications, 1982, p.10). It is interesting to note that Jesus did not come to abrogate the law, but to fulfil, *i.e.* to bring out the essence of the law. The essence of the law is the radical obedience to the will of God, that is loving God and the neighbour. George Wolfang Forell also confirms the fact that Jesus interpreted the law according to its intention. He says, "Jesus does not abolish the law, he affirms it. But it is fulfilled in the light of the new situation. This means that it is interpreted not according to its form (letter) but rather its intention (spirit)". (George Wolfang Forell, *History of Christian Ethics,* Vol. 1: From the New Testament to Augustine, Minneapolis: Augsburg Publishing House, 1979, p.19). According to R.E.O. White, God's Kingdom has two explicit laws—Love God and neighbour—Godward and Manward imperatives of the command love (R.E.O. White, *Biblical Ethics,* Vol.1, Exeter: The Paternoster Press, 1979, p. 82).

The Sermon on the Mount is known as the ethics of the Kingdom. It has placed great emphasis on the purity of the heart. Ladd writes, "Jesus' ethics embody the standard of righteousness that a holy God must demand of men of any age" (George Eidon Ladd, *op.cit*., p.128). Soares Prabhu sees the core demand of the Sermon on loving God and the neighbour. He says , "the Sermon on the Mount, then, is not be read as a collection of precepts (law) but as an invitation to an illustration of the basic Christian attitude of radical obedience (love of God) and radical concern (love of neighbour)." (George M. Soares Prabhu, "The Dharma of Jesus: An Interpretation of the Sermon on the Mount". *Bible Bhashyam* Vol. VI, No.4 (December 1980, p. 370). Commenting on Mathew 5:17-20, Edward Schweizer said, "the crucial point of this section is not to misunderstand Jesus' message: it is the call to take the law seriously, to take God's will seriously" (Edward Schweizer, *The Goodnews According to Mathew*, Atlanta: John Knox Press, 1975, p. 109).

According to Gunther Bornkamm, Jesus' attitude to law is found in his many disputes about the Sabbath. For him, Jesus was against the casuistry developed in Judaism. He feels that Jesus' Commandments were intended not only to avoid murder or adultery but also not to indulge in thinking about it (Gunther Bornkamm, *Jesus of Nazareth*, London: Hodder & Stoughton, 1979, p. 97). Commenting on Mathew 22:34-40 he said: "This twofold commandment of love is the fulfilment and essence of the entire law (Mt.V. 17; vii.12). All other commandments are included in this first and foremost one" (*Ibid*., p.110). About Jesus' understanding on love Bultmann stated, "the requirement for conduct towards others may then be epitomized in the commandment of love. This commandment is generally accepted as essentially Christian requirement, as the new ethic which Jesus taught" (Rudolf Bultmann, *Jesus and the World*, London: Collins, 1958, p. 82). He opines that, for Jesus' love should be applied in the concrete situations of life in which a man encounters other men.

Jesus simplified the Decalogue. According to Ernst Scott, "all the commands are summed up in the two primary demands of love God and love to our fellow-men" (Ernst F. Scott, *The Ethical Teaching of Jesus*, New York: The Macmillan Co., 1925, p. 34). According to Houlden, Jesus brings a greater righteousness transforming the law by adding to its rigour (Mt. 5:20-48). He observes that the concept of loving of God and the neighbour is providing a basis for different issues (J.L. Houlden, *Ethics of the New Testament*, New York: Oxford University Press, 1977, p.49). He made this comment while discussing on Mathew's understanding on Jesus' ethical ideals. According to Bultmann, "the demand for love surpasses every legal demand; it knows no boundary or limit; it holds even in regard to one's enemy (Mt.5:43-48) (Rudolf Bultmann, *Theology of the New Testament*, Vol.1, *op.cit*., p.18). Conzelmann has commented that "the double commandment of love for God and neighbour (Mark 12:28-34) is not new; it is derived from the Old Testament (Deut. 6:4-5; Lev. 19:18). Jesus simply establishes its absoluteness" [Hans Conzelmann, *Jesus* (Reprint), Philadelphia: Fortresss Press, 1975. p. 62]. Love plays a very crucial role in the whole perspective of Jesus on various issues.

The rules on the Sabbath and Jesus' confrontations are also very decisive in Jesus' ethical approach. The conflict stories of the Gospel of Mark (Mark 2:1-3:6) should be given special attention over here. Commenting on Mark 3:3-4, William L. Lane said, "Jesus commanded the man with the withered hand to stand in the midst of the assembled congregation, and posed to his adversaries a rhetorical question: Is it permitted in the Sabbath to do good, or to do harm; to save life or to kill? Formulated in this way, the question demands an answer in terms of the Halakah as determined in scribal study of the law. The tradition clearly asserted that the law was not opposed to saving of life on the Sabbath (William L. Lane, *The Gospel According to Mark*, Michigan: William B. Eerdman's Publishing Company, 1975, p. 123).

About the issue of plucking heads of grain (Mk. 2:23ff), Eduard Schweizer has said, according to Deuteronomy 23:25 it is permissible to pluck the heads of wheat, presumably even on the Sabbath.

Nevertheless, the Pharisees of Jesus' day considered plucking to be part of harvesting, and harvesting on the Sabbath was prohibited (Eduard Schweizer, *The Gospel According to Mark*, London : S.P.C.K., 1978, p. 72). Jesus condemned the practice of keeping the law disregarding the urgent human responsibility and the aspect of doing good. Schweizer comments, 'so far as Jesus is concerned, any obedience which simply follows the letter of the law is less than full obedience, because one can at times fulfil the letter of the law without his heart being in it' (*Ibid*., p.76).

E.P. Sanders has made a very interesting point in relation to the issue of Sabbath. He claims that in the strict sense Jesus did not do any work at all on the Sabbath. He argues, "The stories of healing on the Sabbath (the man with the withered Hand, Matt.12:9-14; Mark 3:1-6; Luke 6:6-1; the woman with the spirit of infirmity, Luke 13:10-17; the healing of a man with Dropsy, Luke 14:1-6) also reveal no instance in which Jesus transgressed the Sabbath law. The matter is quite simple: no work was performed (E.P. Sanders, *Jesus and Judaism*, London SCM Press Ltd., 1985, p. 366).

The synoptic gospels presuppose that the Sabbath rules which were existing on those days were not humane, since they did not cater to the needs of the people. Commenting on Mark 3:1-5, James Dunn writes, that in it Jesus responds to the test case of performing an healing in breach of the Sabbath by healing in breach of the understanding of the Sabbath presupposed by the critical onlookers. As verse 4 sums it up, the question for Jesus was whether doing something which is obviously good can be ruled out on the Sabbath, whether saving life should be treated as merely an exception for the Sabbath (James D.G. Dunn, *Jesus, Paul and the Law: Studies in Mark and Galatians*, Kentucky : Westminster/John Knox Press, 1990, p.23). According to him, Jesus saw the Sabbath laws as something which hindered the human relationships and the mutual responsibility of loving the neighbour (*Ibid*., p.76).

The synoptic Gospels portray this issue of love very vividly. The synoptic Gospels endorse the opinion that law is not against love, but both have a complementary role. A law which does not permit to do good to fellow human beings is to be reformed. It is creative love, the agape, plays the role of the overriding principles in the decision making. Love is for justice, mercy and responsible relationships. Bultmann is right when he remarks, "The demand for love needs no formulated stipulations; the example of the merciful Samaritan shows that a man can know and must know what he has to do when he sees his neighbour in need of his help. The little words 'as yourself' in the love commandment pre-indicate both boundlessness and the direction of loving conduct" (Ernst F. Scott, *op.cit.*, p. 99).

Sex and Marriage

The concept of law and love is related to the issue of sex and marriage. This issue is given much attention in the teaching of Jesus. The so-called antitheses of the Sermon on the Mount (Mt.5:21- 48) also deal with this issue of sex and marriage.

Jesus Christ has related the marriage to the marriage in the creation story. Ernst Scott says, "But the marriage relation is part of the natural order as God Himself designed it; and the sanction involved in it must always remain valid. This idea finds clear expression in the passage (Mt. 19:4-6; Mk. 10:5-9) where Jesus bases his conception of marriage on the creation story" (Ernst F. Scott, *op.cit.*, p. 99).

According to him, the Gospel of Mathew insists on the saving clause that divorce is allowed only on the ground of adultery (Mt. 5:31, 32cf.Mt.9:9), but in Mark's Gospel (10:11,12) divorce is forbidden absolutely (*Ibid.*, pp. 99-100). In the question of divorce and remarriage, Scott brings in a crucial issue that whether Jesus condemned divorce or remarriage. In his own words, "one point is open to question,—whether it was divorce that Jesus condemned or remarriage while husband or wife was still living" (*Ibid*, p.100). It is very clearly stated that the marriage is indissoluble. According to Markan version, Houlden feels that divorces may no longer be tolerated, not because of a new divine decree, but because God has created man for life-long marriage (Mk.10:2f)" (J.L. Houlden, *op.cit.*, p.43).

Jesus was not for regarding women merely as sexual beings, but he was for their dignity as human beings. About the indissolubility of marriage, Schnackenburg observes as he reflected upon Mark 10:2-12; Mathew 19:3-9 and the Sermon on the mount, "Jesus brought two earlier scriptural passages (Gen.1:27; 2:24) into the field against the Mosaic dispensation allowing a bill of divorce to be made out and the woman sent away (Deut. 24:1). From them he argued that the primodial will of God at the beginning of creation intended the indissolubility of marriage" (Rudolf Schnackenburg, *op.cit.*, p. 136).

He states again that "Moses commandment" was given only because of the "hardness of heart" of the Jews, and now the order established at the creation is once again to prevail, so Jesus announces in God's name, What therefore God hath joined together, let not man put asunder" (*Ibid.*, p. 36). He is affirming that Jesus is for indissolubility of marriage. Commenting on the "fornication clauses" (Mt. 5:32 19:9 and Luke 16:18), he said that this does not nullify or relax Jesus' fundamental and universal prohibition of divorce. (*Ibid.*, p.137). It is true that Jesus had never preferred the dissolubility of marriage, but at the same time he could see that there would be cases of divorce. And it is certain that he did not suggest remarriage.

Over this issue the remarks of C.H. Dodd are also important. He feels that in setting forth the teaching, Jesus appeals to the established order of creation as a pointer to the law of God. This he sees clearly in the instance of divorce. He writes that the law of Moses permitted divorce and for Jesus this was only a concession to human obtuseness. He observes, "From the beginning of creation, he created them male and female… and the two are to be one flesh." Hence follows the conclusion "Those whom God has joined, man must not separate (Mark 10:2-9). This is to say, the very nature of man, as created by God, points, if properly understood, to the law of permanent monogamy; and now that the Kingdom of God has come, that aboriginal law must be faced in its full implications" (C.H. Dodd, *Gospel and the Law*, Cambridge: University Press, 1957, p. 79).

Joachim Jeremias has made a good attempt to disclose the idea of Jesus on sex and marriage. He argues that the right to break up a marriage lies with the husband. It is, he says, showing a low estimate of marriage. According to him, the prohibition on divorce (Mark 10:11f; Mt.5:32, 19:9; Luke 16:18) is genuine since Jesus ventures to set himself up against Torah. And he says, the Old Testament permits the discharge of a wife (Deut.24:1) and Judaism followed this practice (Jaochim Jeremias, *op.cit.*, p. 224, *cf.* Gunther Bornkamm feels that Jesus forbids divorce, (*Jesus of Nazareth, op.cit.* p. 99); William A. Heth and Gordon J. Wenham have the opinion that God intends marriage to be indissoluble (Mk. 10:2-9 = Matt. 19:3-8). And, in Jesus understanding, married couples should not separate or divorce, and divorce followed by remarriage constitutes adultery (Matt. 5:32b, Mk. 10:11-12; Lk. 16:18). Divorce, for Jesus is a kind of adultery and leads the woman to commit adultery, except in the case of unchastity (Matt. 5:32) (*Jesus and Divorce: The problem with Evangelical Consensus*, Nashville: Thomas Nelson Publishers, 1984, p.14).

There was a dispute among the Rabbis on this issue (this was among the Hillel and the Shammai school C.B.C. 20). It was over the phrase 'erwat dabar' (Deut. 24:1). "When a man takes a wife and marries her, if she finds no favour in his eyes because he has found some 'erwat dabar' in her, and he writes her a bill of divorcement and puts it in her hand and sends her out of his house". The Shammaites translated the disputed words ('erwat dabar' as 'something shameful' and interpreted in terms of a sexual lapse; the Hillelites separated the two words 'shameful' (and any other) 'thing' and understood by 'thing', e.g. 'If she has let his dinner burn (*Ibid.*, p.225). According to Jeremias the explanation of Shammai school is right; this appears to be sound in the context. It would not be reasonable to think that God's command will allow divorce for any selfish reasons.

John Stott, the New Testament scholar from England has also reflected much over the issue of sex and marriage. Commenting on Mathew 5:27-30 he says, "once again the rabbis were attempting to limit the scope of the commandment *you shall not commit adultery*. Although the sin of desiring another man's wife is included in the tenth commandment against covetousness, they evidently found it more comfortable to ignore this (John R.W. Stott, *op.cit.*, p. 87).

He says that according to the view of the rabbis, they and their pupils kept the seventh commandment, provided that they avoided the adultery itself. They gave also a narrow definition of sexual purity. But Jesus went beyond the perspective of the rabbis and affirmed the true meaning of God's command which was much wider than a mere prohibition of sexual immorality (*Ibid.*, p.87). The teaching of Jesus was against the sex outside marriage whether practiced by married or unmarried people. (*Ibid.*, p.87).

The third antithesis (Mt. 5:31-32) calls for fidelity in marriage. It is also related to Mathew 19:1-9. He explains the word 'unchastity' (Mt. 5:32; 19:9). The word is 'porneia' in Greek which is translated as fornication denoting the immorality of the unmarried, and is often distinguished from moicheia (adultery) which denotes the immorality of the married. Reflecting on the word 'porneia', Stott comments that it is derived from 'porne' which means a prostitute, without specifying whether she (or her client) is married or unmarried (*Ibid.*, p. 97). This does mean that Jesus is against the pre-marital and extra marital sex. Stott argues that the Lord's exposition of the origins of marriage is a divine institution by which God makes permanently one two people who leave their parents in order to form a new unit of society, and he understood from the passages 'become one flesh', 'should not put it asunder' that marriage is, for Jesus, permanent and exclusive.

The synoptic Gospels give the picture on the issue of sex and marriage that sex should not be misused, and it should not be exploited so also marriage. The fidelity in marriage recalls the covenant relationship. It is significant to quote the understanding of William L. Lane on the issue of sex and marriage based on Mark 7:20-23. He tells that 'fornication' is a broad term referring to all acts of sexual immorality which presupposes the breach of marriage of bond and other sexual immorality (William L. Lane, *The Gospel*

According to Mark, Michigan: Wm.B. Eerdmans & Co., 1975, p. 257). Discussing on the issue of Jesus' teaching on the unity and indissolubility of marriage, Fr. Paul Savio Pudussery made three important points which are found in Jesus' teaching (Mk. 10:2-12; Mt. 19:3-12 cf. Mt.5:31-32; Lk. 16-18). In his own words, "He (Jesus) made three important and radical statements: (1) the creation of human kind as man and woman is the foundation for the unity of marriage (Mk. 10:7-9 = Gen. 1:24); (2) marriage unites man and woman so deeply and personally that it cannot be dissolved by the law (Mk. 10:7-9 = Gen 1:27); and (3) a man can be answerable to his own wife as an adulterer (Mk. 10:11; *cf* also Lk.16:18a); formerly, the obligations of a woman to her husband were one-sided, but now they are made mutual; man and woman in marriage are to be seen as equal partners with equal rights and obligations (Fr. Paul S. Pudussery, "Jesus' Teaching on Family Life" in *Bible Bhashyam,* Vol. XVII, No. 4 (December 1991), p. 231. [The bracket is added; and this idea has allusion to Paul Hoffmann "Jesus' saying about Divorce and its interpretation in the New Testament Tradition" *concilium*, Vol. 5, No. 6 (May, 1970), pp. 53-55].

Jesus was looking at the very attitude towards sex as a whole, which has a very important role in relationships. Mathew 5:27-30 point to the very core of the issue. It equates the looking at a girl with lustful eyes with adultery. Edward Schweizer remarks that it recalls the Decalogue which prohibit desiring the neighbour's wife and the concept of God's and marriage with Israel (Hosea 2:4 - 3:1). It calls for fidelity. Schweizer feels that Jesus is also dwelling upon the testament of Issachar (7:2) which declares that even a look can be adulterous. (Eduard Schweizer, *The Goodnews According to Mathew. op.cit*, p.121). Jesus is always concerned of the inner heart and its attitudinal manifestations in our words. In the issue of sex and marriage, the conditioning of the mind according to the directions of God's commandments is extremely significant.

The Ethics of the Fourth Gospel: Selected Issues

It is very clear that the synoptic Gospels and the Gospel of John have similarities and dissimilarities, according to Bultman, "the Gospel of John exhibits the same literary form as the synoptic Gospels" (Rudolf Bultman, *The Gospel According to John: A Commentary* trans. G.R. Beasley-Murray, edited by R.W.N. Hoare and J.K. Richas, Philadelphia: The Westminster Press, 1971, p. 3). But the perspective of these two are different. According to Daniel Harrington, "the synoptic Gospels (Mathew, Mark, Luke) provides a 'common view' (synopsis), but John's perspective is different" (Daniel J. Harrington, *John's Thought and Theology: An Introduction*, Goodnews Series Vol. 33. Willington: Michael Glazier Inc., 1990, p.9). He tells again that the basic theological message of John's Gospel is simple: Jesus, the son of God, reveals the Father. (*Ibid*., p.13). The issues such as law and love, and sex and marriage are not sufficiently dealt with in the fourth Gospel, but it had reflected on these issues to some extent.

Law and Love

The authority and the supremacy of the Revealer is very much evident in the fourth Gospel. Discussing about 1:17, Bultmann commented that it "Stresses the absoluteness of the revelation in Jesus by contrasting it with the law, or to put it in Jewish Christian language, with the Torah, or indeed with the OT as a whole. The question whether there is a positive relationship between the OT and the revelation in Jesus Christ is not here (5:39-47); the evangelist is only concerned with the contrast between the two, which is shown as the contrast between their origin, between Moses and Jesus Christ (Rudolf Bultmann, *The Gospel of John: A commentary, op.cit*., pp.78-79). The elements which are inhuman in the Jewish concept of law was challenged by Jesus as he was for the humane and loving act. John 5:1-18 deals with the attitude of Jesus to the existing Sabbath laws. Here there is no direct attack on Sabbath, but Jesus made a claim that as the Father is working all the time, He is also working. He, in fact, is challenging the inhuman element through this claim. Bultmann states, "thus there is to be not an interruption in the work of Jesus but its cessation. For the present, however, "as long as it is day (9:4), he must work; and in this he is no more restricted by the Sabbath than the Father is" (*Ibid.*, p. 245). From the point of view of the synoptics, the fourth Gospels deals with the issue differently. For the synoptics the question was how far the law of the Sabbath is valid for men and how far it is limited, but for the fourth Gospel the question was whether the law of Sabbath is binding for the Revealer (*Ibid.*, p. 247). Bultmann observes that "The revelation-event means the disruption and negation of traditional religious standards, and their protagonists must become enemies of the Revealer (*Ibid.*, p. 247). Here the fact is that the rules which are unloving and destructive are questioned rather than challenging all the rules and commandments.

Reflecting on the same issue based on the above passage (5:1-18) C.H. Dodd has said that the argument in V.17 makes it different from the synoptics. According to him this has a rabbinic influence, that is the later rabbinic ruling that 'God cannot rest for a moment from the moral government of the universe' (C.H. Dodd, *The Interpretation of the Fourth Gospel*, Cambridge University Press, 1968, p. 323). C.K. Barrett has the opinion that the accusation of illegal activity on the Sabbath recalls no parallel to the reply made by Jesus (V.17) (C.K. Barrett, *The Gospel According to John*, Cambridge University Press, 1968, p.323). The argument that as the Son of God he does what God does is implicit in the synoptic Gospels. Though this is not expressed conspicuously in them (*Ibid.* p.209). But essentially, the challenge Jesus wanted to make in this issue is the same. Daniel Harrington makes an important point in this regard. "The other Gospels base Jesus' free attitude towards the Sabbath rest on his claim that 'the son of man' is lord of the Sabbath" (Mark 2:28; Matt: 12:8; Luke 6:5). Though that statement seems to be in the background of John, it is never said explicitly. Nevertheless, it is possible to understand John 5 as a reflection on its theological implications: As Lord of the Sabbath, Jesus can and must do what God does; therefore, it is appropriate to call him Son of God and equal to the Father (5:18) (Daniel J. Harrington, *op.cit.*, p. 44).

While interpreting John 7:15-24, Bultmann comments, "for John there are no 'dogmatics' without 'ethics' but the love which is demanded of man grows out of faith and cannot exist without it. The consequence of faith is the work of love, because faith is not abstract speculation (neither of course is it the blind acceptance of dogma), but it is the answer to the challenge which is issued in Jesus' word" (Rudolf Bultmann, *The Gospel of John ; A Commentary*, p. 276).

It is true that the circumcision was practiced on the day of the Sabbath as the law of circumcision required that a child be circumcised at the eighth day (Lev. 12:3). It followed that if a child was born on the Sabbath its circumcision fell due also on the Sabbath. It was required that in these circumstances the circumcision should go forward, not withstanding the law of the Sabbath rest). So Jesus was arguing that if the Mosaic law could be broken for circumcision, it is entirely in accord with Moses, intention to break the law to heal the whole man (Rudolf Bultmann, *The Gospel of John: A Commentary*, p. 274). We also see Jesus defending his act of love on Sabbath in John 9:1-41. His argument was that it is now the 'day' and before the day ends, he has to work. This shows the urgency of his mission before the night ('passion' and 'death') comes (Daniel J. Harrington *op.cit.*, p. 61).

The concept of love is very much evident in Jesus' notion of law. The law without love is not appreciated by the Johannine Jesus. That is why the Sabbath rules were challenged. In the Gospel of John the concept of love is explained in a profoundly theological manner. Based on John 3:16, Barrett makes the following comment, "John, however, more than any other writer, develops the conception of love as the nature of God himself and as the means by which the divine life, the relation of the father and the Son, is perpetuated and demonstrated within the community" (13:35) (C.K. Barrett, *op.cit.*, p.180). Jesus had given the 'new' commandment love "one another" as love your 'neighbour' in the synoptic Gospels (Jn. 13:34). According to Daniel Harrington, 'At any rate, the loving service of others will keep alive the spirit of Jesus'. What is imagined is a 'chain' of loving services: 'As I have loved you, so you also should love one another' (13:34) (Daniel J. Harrington, *op.cit*, p. 83). According to him Jesus' reply (14:23-24) reveals that Father and Son are present where love for Jesus and fidelity to his teaching are present (*Ibid*., p.87). The roots for the love are found in the self-sacrificing love of Jesus (*Ibid*., p. 90). The eternal love between the Father and Son and the obedience to the Father's will are to be reproduced by the followers, that is what Jesus expected (C.H. Dodd, *The Interpretation of the Fourth Gospel, op.cit*., p. 405).

The Commandment of Jesus to love one another has tremendous amount of communal implications. Loving God should be reflected in our lives through our relationships with others. According to Barrett, the love is to have its ground and its norm in the love received from Jesus (C.K. Barrett, *The Gospel According to John*, p. 543). The synoptics and the Fourth Gospel do not contradict each other in the issue of law and love though these Gospels have their own way of argument and development of the theme. Love is the overriding norm and the law should be evaluated in the context of what is loving , constructive, creative and human.

Sex and Marriage

We have no much material in the Gospel of John on this theme. But there are references about the issue of sex and marriage in this Gospel. According to Fr. Paul Savio Pudussery, "Jesus held marriage in high esteem and this is evident from the fact that he blessed a marriage at Cana with his presence and support (*cf.* Jn.2:1-11) [Paul. S. Pudussery 'Jesus' Teaching on Family Life', *Bible Bhashyam,* Vol. XVII, No. 4 (December 1991)] p. 230. In chapters 4 and 8, we see two clear instances on sex and marriage issue.

In the fourth chapter of the Fourth Gospel, the discourse with the Samaritan woman, Jesus reveals her immoral life. William Hendrickson comments on John 4:19 that 'the woman does not deny the remarks of Jesus concerning her immoral life. In fact, by calling him a prophet (which is to her meant one who can read secrets) that this stranger's resume of her evil conduct shocked her beyond words (William Hendrickson, *The Gospel of John*, Pennsylvania: The Banner of Truth Trust, 1976, p. 165).

Mathew Vellanical, the well-known scholar in Johannine studies also made some valuable observation in this context. He feels that the Samaritan woman was suddenly aware of her looseness and immorality and was frightened, and she had played a defensive mechanism 'I have no husband' (Mathew Vellanical, *Studies in the Gospel of John*, Bangalore: Asian Trading Corporation, 1982, p. 91). Though she did not make a public confession, she had realized her sins. This is obvious from her understanding of Jesus as a prophet and her commitment to the Messiah.

Daniel Harrington states that according to Lev. 20:10 and Deuteronomy 22:22-24 the punishment for adultery is supposed to be death. Stoning was the mode of capital punishment and the first stone would be thrown by the witnesses (Dt. 17:17). The aim of the Pharisees was to test Jesus whether he would be faithful to the letter of the Mosaic law (Daniel J. Harrington, *op.cit.* p. 56). The comment based on John 8:1-11 is quite useful. Jesus was questioning the integrity of the people who brought them. It reveals the fact that they are also not clear in the moral life. The sexual immorality was challenged by Jesus. Jesus did not condone the sin of the woman also. Daniel Harrington writes, "He forgives the sinner without condoning sin, thus preserving the delicate balance between justice and mercy that it is characteristic of biblical tradition" (*Ibid.*, p. 56).

The perspective on sex and marriage presented in Gospel of John is very significant. It does not give any room for immorality and loose sex. The family and the chastity in life are endorsed. From the instances of the fourth Gospel, it is very clear that the human beings are reminded to keep the moral standards. The Samaritan woman was reminded of her personal life in relation to sex and marriage. The woman who was caught in adultery was asked to correct herself from the present style of life.

The 'law and love' issue plays a very dominant role in the Gospels' ethics. It is quite true to say that Jesus had questioned the interpretation of the rabbis which were very legalistic. They had interpreted the law disregarding the essence of the law, which is love. Law is understood by Jesus to enhance the love and life among the human beings in their relationships. Love is the overriding norm in the ethical methodology of Jesus Christ. The love that is expressed in the Father-Son (Father God and Jesus Christ) relationship is the supreme example to be followed. The key phrases may be 'love God', 'love your neighbour as thyself' and 'love one another'. The law was neither understood in a rigid absolutistic term in the Gospels nor in a complete relativitistic manner without any parameters.

The rigid and inhuman Sabbatical rules were challenged by Jesus as he broke them. He did it in order to show that the loveless rules are less important than mercy and justice. The law and love are not contradictory, since the essence of law is love. And there can be no law without love. Love is not without principles. The love is not without any content. The love as a norm is guided by the Kingdom values. Love is regulated by justice, righteousness, mercy and other virtues. Love is God-oriented, Christ-oriented and the scripture-oriented. The love that we found in the teaching of Jesus and the Gospels is not arbitrary.

Sex and marriage is another significant issue. The covenant fidelity which is rooted in the Old Testament term 'hesed' which plays a very dominant role in this regard. Sex is not to be misused before or after marriage. The pre-marital and extra-marital sex are condemned by the Gospels. The homosexuality, lesbianism and the like are not condoned by Jesus. The loose sex is not at all tolerated by Jesus. The ethics of the Gospels reveal that the adultery, prostitution and other forms of loose sex are not condoned. Sex is to be responsibly used in the family (husband-wife) relationship. In the Fourth Gospel, we see Jesus revealed the sin of the Samaritan woman and also he told the woman caught in adultery to 'sin no more'. Even looking at a girl with lustful heart is condemned by Jesus.

Marriage is instituted by God and it should be kept responsible. It is understood as indissoluble. The divorce and re-marriage are not affirmed by Jesus in his teachings. Marriage is to be kept sacred and the sanctity of marriage plays a vital role in building up a stable society. Jesus rejected the divorce and he inclined to the view of Shammai School rather than Hillel School, which allowed divorce even in the case of trivial matters. Jesus was bringing in the creation model in this regard. The affirmation of the monogamy and the idea of indissoluble bond (let not man put it asunder) are the key implications. In the marriage issue, Jesus was having an uncompromising stand. He considered the idea of issuing divorce certificate (Moses also sanctioned it in some cases) as *null* and *void*, since it was not related to the spirit of the law. It was done by Moses because of the hardened heart of the people. Breaking of marriage bond is permitted by Jesus only in the case of unchastity, *i.e.* the infidelity (adultery/extra-marital sex). And it is presumed that those who have divorced should remain unmarried. These principles are very stringent, but it discloses how God is concerned of the responsible relationship within the family. He foresees the consequences of divorce which harm the stability of meaningful existence. Though Jesus was stressing normative rules, he also recognized the importance of evaluative approach.

7

Situation Ethics: Fletcher's Perspective

Introduction

In the 1960s the situation ethics emerged as a shock to the existing ethical systems. John A.T. Robinson, James Pike and Joseph Fletcher are the prominent figures in the area of situationism. Joseph Fletcher is, of course, the most important figure because he has reflected so much on this issue than anyone else. Thus, he became the synonym of situation ethics. Joseph Fletcher was born, according to Erickson, in New York, New Jersey, April 10, 1905. He received his B.A. from the University of West Virginia and B.D. from Berkeley Divinity School and also studied at Yale and London. He is the most Influential spokesman of situation ethics (Millard J. Erickson, "Fletcher, Joseph" Baker's *Dictionary of Christian Ethics*, edited by Carl F. Henry, U.S.A. *Baker Book House Company*, 1973, p. 247).

The Background of the Emergence of Situation Ethics

There are several elements that influenced the emergence of situation ethics. The criticisms between Joseph Fletcher and the eminent ethicist Paul Ramsey will enable us to have some idea on the influence. Fletcher condemns legalism and the universally valid rules. [Harvey Cox, *The Situation Ethics Debate* (Philadelphia, The Westminster Press, 1966), p. 250, Hereafter Cox, *Debate*]. Ramsey claims that Fletcher is highly arbitrary, antinomian and relative [Paul Ramsey, *The Deeds and Rules in Christian Ethics* (New York: Charles Seribner's Sons, 1967), p.199; Hereafter Ramsey, *Deeds*]. It seems that Fletcher is against the absolute moral norms. Quoting Fletcher, Ramsey has said that the antinomians and existentialists follow no forecastable cause from one situation to another (*Ibid.*, p. 164). For Ramsey, Fletcher's ethical method is act-agapism, and according to Frankena, act-agapism never appeals to rules (William K. Frankena, *Ethics*, New Delhi: Prentice-Hall of India, 1988, p. 56; Hereafter Frankena, *Ethics*).

Fletcher is influenced by the utilitarianism, evolutionism, positivism and even some other philosophical trends. The situationism is totally against the deontological method, along with that the natural law tradition and Roman Catholic morality. The ethical understanding of Quakers and puritans are in the background of the emergence of situational ethics. Fletcher condemned the protestant ethics for its puritanical rigid rules [Joseph Fletcher, *Situation Ethics* (Philadelphia, The Westminster Press, 1966) p.19; Herafter Fletcher, *Situation*].

The Sophists

In the fifth century B.C. the sophists were lived in Greece. For them 'man is the measure of all things'. Man can decide for himself, says William Lillie, what is right and what is wrong, and there is no other standard [William Lillie, *An Introduction to Ethics* (New Delhi : Allied Publishers Ltd., 1989) p. 93; Hereafter Lillie, *An Introduction to Ethics*]. According to Lillie, the more revolutionary among their thought was that all morality was a matter of human convenience, and that we call things good merely because they suit ourselves or the majority of mankind (*Ibid.*, p. 93).

Heraclitus, the sophist has said, "No man step into the same river twice, for fresh waters are ever upon him" [Norman Giesler. *Options in Contemporary Christian Ethics* (Michigan : Book House, 1991) p.10]. The sophist ethics presuppose that the context is all the time changing so also the moral decisions.

Hedonism

According to Giesler, "The epicureans gave impetus to a relativistic ethics by making pleasure the essence of good and pain the essence of evil" (*op. cit,* p. 11). Pleasure is central to the hedonistic ethics. Lillie explains that, "Ethical hedonism holds that pleasantness is the only quality because of which an experience is good or valuable. A good action is an action which leads to a pleasant experience as its consequence, and the right action at any moment is the one which will lead to more pleasant experiences, or as we commonly say, to greater pleasure than any other action which is possible for the agent at that particular moment" (Lillie, *An introduction to Ethics*, p. 161).

Skepticism

Skepticism does not make any firm conclusions. According to Giesler, "In ethics, this would mean one should never consider anything an absolutely or universally right or wrong" (*Ibid*., p. 12).

Nominalism

It goes with the name of William of Ockham. He denied the existence of universals. Ockham stresses the importance of the intuitive awareness of particular things which paves away for a personalistic ethics (Collison, Diane. *Fifty Major Philosophers: A Reference Guide*. London: Croom Helm, 1987. p. 41). This has enabled to become situational in ethical decision-making.

Utilitarianism

Jeremy Bentham (1748—1832) and John Stuart Mill are the significant names in the utilitarianism. They are quite related to hedonism. In the words of Giesler, "Jeremy Bentham (1748—1832) laid down the principle that one should act so as to produce the greatest good for the greatest number in the long run" (*op. cit*, p. 15).

The action that may produce good results for a time will not be best for all persons. So it brings relativism so also the situationism. Giesler understands that "Utilitarian relativism implies that the end can justify any means" (*Ibid.*, p. 16). Happiness is the sum of pleasure for them, says Anthony Quinton.

According to Quinton, "Utilitarianism is a combination of two principles:

1. The consequentialist principle that the rightness or wrongness of an action is determined by the goodness or hardness of the results that flow from it, and
2. The hedonist principle that the only thing that is good in itself is pleasure and the only thing bad in itself is pain" [Anthony Quinton, *Utilitarian Ethics* (London : Macmillan Press, 1973), p.1; Hereafter Quinton, *Utilitarian*].

For Frankena, "Fletcher's situation ethics is a modified act-agapism, but he gives it a clearly act-utilitarian and teleological twist (Quinton, *Utilitarian*, p. 1). Act-agapism is against absolute rules. The act-utilitarianism would not permit to use any rules or generalization from past experience (Frankena, *Ethics*, p. 37). Situationism is more related to act-utilitarianism.

Mill argues that principles or morals should promote happiness (*Ibid.*, p. 36). Lillie has tried to summarize John Stuart Mill's arguments in the following statements:

(a) Pleasure is the only thing that is desirable;
(b) The only proof that a thing is desirable is the fact that people do actually desire it;
(c) Each person's own pleasure or happiness is a good to that person, so the general happiness is good to everybody;
(d) Men do desire other objects, that they desire them as a means to pleasure; and
(e) If one of two pleasures is preferred by those who are competently acquainted with both we are justified in saying that this preferred pleasure is superior in quality to the other (Quinton, *op.cit.*, p. 2).

Evolutionalism

T.H. Huxley (1825-1895) and Julian Huxley (1887-1975) have worked out an evolutionary ethic. Giesler says, "the central tenet of evolutionary ethics is that right is what aids the evolutionary development of mankind and wrong that hinders it" (Lillie, *op.cit.*, p.167). Julian Huxley's principle is, says Giesler, that it is right to respect human individuality and to encourage its fullest development.

Emotivism

A.J. Ayer (1910-1970) argued that ethical statements are emotive. In Giesler's words, for Ayer, "Ethics is not prescriptive; it is simply emotive. Ethical pronouncement are merely ejaculations of our subjective feelings and not divine imperatives about moral duty" (Giesler, *op.cit.*, p. 17).

Positivism

Positivism affirms that only that which is observed can be believed. It does not approve traditional conventions and pre-determined rules. The situationism is influenced by positivism. According to Joseph Vadackumcherry, "Situationism is bound up with a theological positivism in which faith propositions are posited or affirmed voluntaristically rather than rationalistically" (*op.cit*, p. 18).

Humanism

According to Roser Hazelton, Humanist Ethics finds in freedom the signal instance of man's unique, even 'absurd' standing in the total universe, as known in the natural science. It seeks to preserve and protect that freedom by asserting man's independence from natural conditioning on the one hand and from supernatural or divine sovereignty on the other [Joseph Vadackumcherry, *Natural-Law Morality Versus Situationism in Morals* (Cochin : Louis Memorial Press, 1969) p. 66; Hereafter Vadackumcherry, *Natural Law*, p. 83). He continued to say, "that man can know, seek, and realize his own good without reliance upon any standard external to himself, is the hallmark of humanist ethics" (Roser Hazelton, "Humanism and Humanitarianism", *Dictionary of Christian Ethics* edited by John Macquarrie, London, SCM Ltd., 1967, p. 158; hereafter Macqurrie, *Dictionary*).

Cultural Relativism

The modern cultural and anthropological analysis argue for a relativism. "Relativism" for Harold Kuhn, is a theory that the basis for judgements in knowledge, culture, or ethics differs according to persons, events or situations. It connotes a state of mind or a way of thinking inhospitable to absolute claims. (*Ibid.*, p.158). The present cultural studies argue that the values found in one culture cannot be universalized. The cultural relativism centres in the rejection of universal norms (Harold B. Kuhn, "Relativism" Baker's *Dictionary of Christian Ethics* edited by Carl F. Henry. Michigan: Baker Book House, 1981 p. 572; Hereafter Henry, *Baker's*). Kuhn states that, moral or ethical relativism is a specialized form of cultural relativism in which any universally acceptable criterion for measuring values is rejected. All value systems are viewed as being of equal validity, since they are all culturally conditioned and determined (*Ibid.*, p. 573). The arguments is that no value can be found true in all contexts.

Existentialism

Soren Kierkegaard and Jean-Paul Sartre (1906-1978) are the two important existentialists. According to Joseph Fletcher, 'Sartre refuses to admit any *generally* valid principles at all, nothing even ordinarily valid, to say nothing of universal laws' (Lillie, *An Introduction to Ethics*. p. 102). In the words of Carl Michalson, "living by laws, which is a way of knowing what to do, is regarded by existentialist as 'bad faith' (Sartre and Simon de Beavoir)" (Fletcher, *Situation*, p. 25). He continued to say that, "any abridgement of human freedom is 'bad faith'. A legalistic ethic abridges freedom by taking tensions out of the hands of the responsible selves" (Carl Michalson, "Existentialist Ethics"; *Dictionary* by Macquarrie, p. 124). For existentialist ethics, freedom surpasses all laws. Freedom is understood as a source of man's possibility to act ethically (*Ibid.*, p. 124).

While Sartre was a rational existentialist, Kierkegard was a religious existentialist. It is important to understand the latter's 'teleological suspension of the ethical' Carl Michalson explains: "Openness to the future has primacy over conformity to the past. To use Sartre's term, one simply 'nihilates' which is to say, 'suspends' it, in order to let the demands of the future emerge. The past tells a man what he ought to do. The future is a reliable guide simply because it does not tell a man what to do, but appeal to him to 'invent' or create' in the light of the emerging situation" (*Ibid.*, p.124). The existentialism brings a radical subjectivism and personalism in ethics. Sartre believed that there is no place of objective meaning or value to life (*Ibid.*, p.124). It leads to antinomianism too.

Joseph Vadackumcherry also tried to explain the existentialist ethics. He said: "Since the existentialists are so concerned with individual morality, they tend to present it concretely rather than abstractly" (*Ibid.*, p. 19). This is the special feature of existentialistic treatment of morality. Since there is discontinuity of one situation or moment of experience from another, the existentialists are against generalities (Vadackumcherry, *Natural-Law*, p. 66). There is also personalism in existentialism. "For Sartre the key to man's moral life is his freedom. In a world without God, human person is an absolute value that cannot be subordinated to anything else" (*Ibid.*, p.67). For Sartre, freedom is the only source of value (*Ibid.* pp. 68-69).

Puritans and Quakers

The Puritans and the Quakers were the two movements from England. Fletcher condemns the legalistic Puritanism. Richard Baxter (1615-91) typifies the puritan mind. One of the characteristics of puritan life is sobriety. It does not approve any loose sex. According to Waldo and Niebuhr, "when the puritan calls on men to be sober, he is simply reminding them that this life is swift and solemn trust, an arena of crucial decision, wherein the high values of the religious life are in competition with the cheap, and easy values of world's pleasures" [Dario Composta. *Moral Philosophy and Social Ethics* (Bangalore:Theological Publications in India, 1988), p.37]. The puritans are keeping very rigid rules on sex and the pleasures. Pleasure seeking is ungodly for them. Worldliness is understood as the chief enemy of morality.

The Quaker movement will go after the name of George Fox (1624-1691). He called the people to repentance and directed them to the inner light. He appealed to a new kind of authority which is not the church or scripture but the inward authority of experience. [Waldo Beach and Richard Niebuhr eds, *Christian Ethics: Sources of living tradition*, 2nd edn. (New York: Alfred A. Knopf, 1973) p. 302]. The Quakers felt the indwelling presence of the spirit of God. They believed in the inward change rather than the outward symbol. Fox they discovered an inner spiritual experience and a strong sense of an immediate and direct relation to God [Marjorie Sykes. *Quakers in India* (London : George Allen & Unwin, 1980), p. 5].

Natural Law Tradition

The natural law tradition is usually understood as a system in which natural orders and universal rules are affirmed. It is deontological in character. According to Vadackumcherry, "the sum and summit of natural law consists in a few most general or universal principles (*viz.* "man should embrace good and avoid evil")" [Gorman H. George "The society of Friends" *Our church and why we believe in them* (London: Seeley, Service & Co. Ltd., 1961), p. 218]. Situationism is deadly against natural law and deontological ethics. The Roman Catholic morality is influenced by the natural law. For Thomas Aquinas, "law is nothing but the dictate of practical reason issued by a soverign who governs a complete community" (Vadackumcherry, *Natural Law*, p. 33). In the Anglican ethics also the natural law doctrine has found a firm place [Robin Gill, *A Text Book of Christian Ethics*. (Edinburg: T & T Clark Ltd., 1985), p.76]. Duncan B. Forrester has quoted Cicero to convey the idea of natural law: "True law is right reason in agreement with nature; it is of universal application, unchanging and it avert from wrong doing by its prohibitions" [Karl H. Peschke, Christian *Ethics,* Vol. 1, (Bangalore: TPI, 1987), p.134]. This statement confirms the deontological dimension of the natural law. It also points out the universality of natural law.

'Thomas Aquinas (1225-1274) taught that the natural law is ordained by God, and that it is concerned with the social life of man as a creature of time and space living in the actual world where all his social relations are to be ordered according to the law of God' says Lillie [Quoted from *De Republica* 3-12, 33 by Duncan B. Forrester *Religion and Society* Vol. XI, No. 4 (Dec. 1964), p. 29]. For Aquinas, says Lillie, "Natural law is a judgement teaching what is right, a judgement necessarily following from the Divine being, and unalterably determined by the nature of things as they exist in God" (Lillie, *An Introduction to Ethics*, p.141).

Conclusion

It is very clear that there are several influences behind the emergence of situation ethics. The reaction to natural law tradition, pietism and deontological ethics, and the affirmation of cultural relativism, the philosophies such as existentialism, the utilitaranism, skepticism and nomianlism played a dominant role in the formation of situation ethics. Situationism moved away from the absolute rules to relativism. It denies the absolutes. The influences have made situationism personalistic ethics. The universal rules are rejected by it.

The Main Concepts in the Ethical Thought of Joseph Fletcher

Love, sexuality and marriage, reproduction, birth control and dignity of life and stewardship are identified as the important concepts in the ethical thought of Joseph Fletcher.

Love

The situationism of Fletcher is rooted on love and it rejects the rules. He tells that situationists are commanded to love people and not principles [Joseph Fletcher, "Why New?" *Religion in Life* Vol. XXXV, No. 2 (Spiring, 1966), p. 188.]. He further states that the only absolute of new morality is agapeic or loving neighbour-concern, and it seeks the good of the people by decisions tailored to the relativists of each particular situation (*Ibid*, p. 188). He argues that situationism is against *a priori* rules [Joseph Fletcher, "Love and Utility" *the Christian Century*,Vol. XCV, No. 20 (May 31, 1978), p. 592]. For him, principles and norms are contingent and they are valid only if they serve love in any situation (Joseph Fletcher, Situation, p.30). He feels that the rules will reduce persons into objects. The fixed rules are not appropriate in the situation of decision-making. The absolute moral norms which are rooted in principles are unacceptable to him.

The love, in his opinion, is antithetical to rules. Only love is intrinsically good and love is against prescriptive rules. He is not in favour of universally valid rules and legalism. Legalism in Christian tradition, says Fletcher, has two forms: one is based on reason and natural law (Roman Catholic tradition) which argues for universally valid moral rules, and the other is based on scripture (Protestants) and argues like the Roman Catholics for universally valid rules (*Ibid.*, p. 21). The criticism of Paul Ramsey over Fletcher is that, "in actual fact Fletcher's operating ethical method is an extreme and exclusive act-agapism; if not antinomian, it is certainly anomie, no matter how he formally defines situation ethics and attempts to locate in between extremes" (Paul Ramsey, *Deeds*, p.148).

Joseph Fletcher proposes that the circumstances will alter rules and principles, and situation ethics is not rule-oriented, but fact-oriented, data conscious, inquiring and anti-legalistic. For Fletcher love is only universal, and it might only always good in all situations. In his words, love is the only universal. But love is not something we have or are, it is something we do. Unlike the other you might mention, love alone when well served is always good and right in every situation (*Ibid.*, pp. 60-61).

Fletcher's 'agape' will take any shape in the situation which is beyond any prediction. He sees the new morality as a departure from moral law and prescriptive rules to love and people. This is explicated by him in propositions:

(a) We are commanded to love people and not principles, so that the needs of human beings come before adherence to rules is often less opposed to human welfare than sentimental or un-reflective persons may be willing to appreciate, and

(b) We are to love people and use things, "things" including abstractions thus reducing them from subjects to objects (Joseph Fletcher, 'What's in a Rule? A situationist's view. *Norm and Context in Christian Ethics* edited by Gene H. Outka and Paul Ramsey, London: SCM Press, 1968, p. 328; hereafter Outka & Ramsey, *Norm and Context*).

He presupposes that the principles are unloving, and they are not person-oriented but reduce subjects into objects.

In this four working principles (pragmatism, relativism, positivism and personalism), he emphasized the role of love. Fletcher argued that the pragmatism threw away fixed principles and abstracts and their actions will be based on what is concrete and practical and not on the basis of what is right and wrong (Joseph Fletcher, *Situation,* p. 43). For him the four working principles are providing ample room for love in ethical decision-making.

It is also important to look into the six propositions of Fletcher. The first proposition is "only one thing is intrinsically good; namely love; nothing else at all". He argues that value exists only in reference to person, and good and bad depends on the situation. The second proposition is, "the ruling norm of Christian decision is love; nothing else". Fletcher asserts that the last six commands of Decalogue (filial piety, command against killing, false witness, adultery, stealing and covetousness) are not law of love, but love of law (*Ibid*., p.74). The third proposition of Fletcher is, "Love and Justice are the same, for justice is the love distributed, and nothing else". He defines justice as giving to each one what is one's due, so also is love for him (*Ibid.*, p. 90). The fourth proposition is, "Love wills the neighbours' good whether we like him or not". He opines that Christian love is not sentimental and so the radical obligation of love includes even the enemy or the one who is not our friend [Joseph Fletcher, *Moral Responsibility: Situation Ethics at Work*, (Philadelphia : The Westminster Press, 1967), p. 21; Hereafter Fletcher, Moral]. The fifth prepositions of Fletcher is that "only the end justifies the means; nothing else" (Fletcher, *Situation,* p. 120). He states that the legalists rationalize war's ruthless method of forcing, killing, surgical mutilations and capital punishment, and his argument is that no rule can be made to abide by all in all situations.

In the sixth preposition that "love's decisions are made situationally, not prescriptively", Fletcher provides two incidents which seems to be different, but he justifies both (*Ibid.*, p. 134). The first one is as follows: In 1841 a ship 'William Brown' out of Liverpool to Philadelphia, struck an iceberg and began to sink. The captain, seven seamen and thirty two passengers were in a boat, which was double of what that boat could carry. The rough sea doomed them. The mate ordered most of the males into the sea. They refused, but Holmes, a seamen, pitched them out. In Philadelphia, Holmes was convicted of murder. In Fletcher's opinion, legalism says Holmes did an evil thing but "situation ethics says it was bravely sinful, it was a good thing" (*Ibid.*, p. 136).

Fletcher tells another story: when captain Scott's expedition to south pole ran into trouble and they were making it back to the coast with no time to spare, one of his men was injured and had to be carried. The stretcher would slow them down dangerously. Scott decided to stick with the men and they are all perished. Fletcher's characteristic argument is that we can't predict the future, so a decision taken in a particular moment of time regardless of past or future is authentic (*Ibid.*, p. 136). Paul Ramsey observed that Fletcher's situation ethics is arbitrary subjectivism (Ramsey, *Deeds*, pp. 218-19).

Fletcher's situationism centred around the concept of love which is totally against the prefabricated rules or principles. It takes any form in accordance with the situation. His concept of love denies the *a priori* rules and it is allergic to law. He absolutized the love but the content of love is not clear.

Sexuality and Marriage

The sexuality and marriage is another important concept in the ethical thinking of Fletcher. Sex can be understood in the light of dynamic psychology and anthropology, as the whole sphere of action and feeling dominated by the relations between men and women; a pervasive force in all aspects of human personality, says Fletcher. [Joseph Fletcher, "A moral philosophy of Sex" *Sex and Religion* Today edited by Simon Doniger (New York: Association Press, 1953), p.187]. Fletcher feels that the New Testament is strikingly fragmentary in the treatment of sex problems and ethics: "Jesus, for example, had nothing whatever to say about courtship, perversions, masturbation, sex manners, codes of reproduction and parenthood, multiple marriage, incest, birth control, artificial insemination, foeticide and the like" (*Ibid.*, p. 187).

Fletcher argues that Jesus' whole sex ethic is rooted in his insistence on the prohibition of looking at woman with lustful eye. He also condemns the traditional Christian understanding of sex as inherently evil. He admonishes the use of the sexual partner as an object and engaging in sadistic practices which inflict pain (*Ibid.*, p.192). Though he rejects the object-subject relationship in sexual act and the sexual offenses, he justifies the different kinds of sex (heterosex, homosexuality and auto or masturbation) saying that they can be evil or good depends on whether love is fully served. He also agrees with extramarital sex if it serves love. This is clear from *Mrs. Bergmeiers' case* (she was imprisoned and she wanted to join her family. The only way is to get pregnant and have the release. She approached a sympathetic jailor and was conceived. She was released for joining the family) (Fletcher, *Situation,* p. 165). He does not find any infidelity in that case. The extra-marital sex over her is understood by him as a loving act.

Fletcher is not against homosexuality and pre-marital sex. He agrees with Leo Koch's opinion that sexual intercourse should be condoned among sufficiently mature to engage in it without social consequence and without violating their own codes of morality and ethics, with due regard for the three qualifying factors—maturity, social concern and integrity (Fletcher, *Moral*, p. 129). He holds that the view that Bible affirms sex as a high order value with the claim that Bible talks about sex solely within marriage is only an inference (*Ibid.*, p. 134). He argues that there is nothing explicitly in the Bible forbidding pre-marital sexual acts. "Only extra-marital acts, *i.e.*, adultery are forbidden" (*Ibid.*, p.134). He brings a case in order to justify pre-marital sex. He states, "A young unmarried couple might decide, if they make their decisions to have intercourse (*e.g.*, by getting pregnant to force a selfish parent to relent his overbearing resistance to their marriage) (Fletcher, *Situation,* p. 104). According to Ramsey, Fletcher's perspective that any kind of sex can be judged as good or evil depends upon whether love is served ignore the problem of constructing an ethics of some or of any sort in areas of human life that have important social dimensions (Ramsey, *Deeds*, p. 153).

Fletcher does not disregard any sexual act with mutual consent. His concept of sexuality found every sexual act as loving if it is done with mutual consent. Though he condemns the sexual offenses, he does not understand the fact that the sexual promiscuity will lead to sexual offenses and object-subject relationship. He also permits divorce if that will best serve the emotional and spiritual welfare of parents and children in a particular family (Fletcher, *Situation*, p. 104). He failed to realize the fact that the divorce will never bring emotional and spiritual welfare, rather it breaks them all. Fletcher's concept of sexuality and marriage are not very normative, but evaluative.

Reproduction

Fletcher blames the English law which validates marriage only by sexual union (*Ibid.*, p. 79). He favours the Artificial Insemination by Doner (AID), Artificial Insemination by Husband (AIH) and surrogate mother. The artificial insemination, says Fletcher, should not be forbidden since it could not be God's will or man's that a married couple should be condemned to childlessness and hold on to an unproductive love merely because of psychological or biological accident (*Ibid.*, p. 118). The A.I.D. and A.I.H. are, for him, the means to overcome the emotional strain and frustrations in married life. [Joseph Fletcher, *Morals and Medicine*. (Boston : Beacon Press, 1965), p. 101; Hereafter Fletcher, *Morals and Medicine*]. The test-tube babies are not beyond the framework laid by Fletcher.

He explains that the A.I.D. is not adultery. Quoting levirate system of the Old Testament, he said that the artificial Insemination by Donor is not adultery. [Stephen E. Lammers and Allen Verhey ed. *On Moral Medicine*. (Michigan: William B. Eerdman's Publishing Co., 1987) p. 348; hereafter Lammers & Verhey, *On Moral*]. His concept is that using all possible means to overcome the frustrations in married life when the husband or wife suffers from disorders. In Fletcher's outlook the third party sperm and ova or graft gonads which can overcome childlessness should not be categorized as adultery. "Adultery cannot apply any longer to the donations of due powers of our 'loins' to persons in need just because they are not one's spouse" (*Ibid*, p. 348). His understanding of marriage covenant and the reproduction are quite alien to the biblical understanding. He strongly believes that every one should help our friends and neighbours if they need to share our productivity (*Ibid*, p. 353). He urges to make use of all medical devices to overcome sterility.

He favours the cloning and screening with some reservations. He says, "good reasons in general for cloning are that it avoids genetic diseases, bypasses sterility, predetermines an individual's gender, and preserves family likenesses" (*Ibid*, p. 353). He justifies cloning in the situation of meeting a family's survival need. (Joseph Fletcher, "Ethical Aspects of Genetic Control" *Bioethics* edited Thomas A.Shannon (New York: Paulist Press, 1976), p.333]. In Screening and the consequent abortion is approved by him for bringing up a community without physical and other genetic diseases or defects (Lammers & Verhey, *op.cit.* p. 360). He is for the reproduction without any defects.

The reproduction is not necessarily the result a physical union between the husband and wife for Fletcher. He does not see any problem in bringing forth the children through any artificial means. He has found that enabling people to overcome sterility is a common responsibility of humanity and it is essential part of loving neighbour. He has a very relative understanding of marital fidelity and covenant.

Birth Control

The Roman Catholic church's faith in the natural law has ended up in declaring contraception and sterilization as against nature. Fletcher argues that this understanding will forbid love making which is a vital part in marriage (Fletcher, *Moral*, p. 31). He rejects the catholic moral claim of 'killing' the life in the case of contraception. (Fletcher, *Morals* and *Medicines*, p. 89). For him, contraception enables us to have planning of family. In the issue of sterilization, Fletcher has commented that the natural law moralists are trapped into cheating on love or even altogether denying love's demands (Fletcher, *Situation*, p. 80).

The use of the devices for birth control, for Fletcher, is a matter of personal freedom and responsibility (Joseph Fletcher. "The ethics of genetic control: some answers" in *On Moral Medicine* edited by Lammer & Verhey, p. 360). He rejects the irresponsible sterilization which denies the obligation to propagate (*Ibid.*, p. 360). For him birth control is a wise and moral act. According to him, the birth control enables us to have a better community, since the contraception and sterilization can be used for therapeutic reasons. It keeps us away from the birth of the genetically defective children. (Fletcher, *Morals and Medicine*, p. 160). The birth control serves love and it becomes a blessing for the good of humanity in the view of Fletcher.

Fletcher approves the punitive nature of sterilization which is to punish the sex offender or to make it impossible for him to repeat offence (*Ibid.*, p. 145). Fletcher's concept of birth control is very much grounded on love's demands which is an integral idea in his ethical thought. He sees everything with "love" and "concern" which is rooted in relativism and freedom.

Dignity of Life

Fletcher's concept of dignity of life is quite different from the Roman Catholic understanding. In order to identify his concept of dignity of life, it is important to know his notion of humanhood. In his perspective, in order to be human, human beings have to be something more than biologically classifiable as organism of the species *homo sapiens*. In order to be human, he says, they should have an individual or separate existence and a functioning cerebral cortex, that is, some minimal level of intelligence. So Fletcher infers that "therefore an individual of the species who is not yet human, a fetus, and one who is ceased to be a "brain dead" patient, is without the status of being human or human being" (Fletcher, "The Ethics of Genetic Control: some answers" *On Moral Medicine* edited by Lammers & Verhey, p. 356). Fletcher underlines the fact that the key to humanness is the neocortical function.

Fletcher has proposed fifteen positive criteria and five negative criteria to indicate humanhood. The positive criteria are as follows: (1) Minimal intelligence—according to Fletcher an individual of the species of *homo sapiens* who falls below the IQ 40-mark in a standard Stanford-Binet is a person, below 20-mark and therefore, is not a person [Joseph Fletcher, "Indicators of Humanhood : A Tentative Profile of Man", *Bioethics* edited by Thomas A. Shannon (New York: Paulist Press, 1970), p. 320]. 20-mark is regarded as necessary for minimal intelligence and it is essential for decision-making, for Fletcher. (2) Self-awareness-self-consciousness is absent in lower vertebrates as well as in the non-vertebrates. The irreversible damage to the brain cortex may lead to non-self awareness or unconsciousness. For Fletcher, this has to do with the judgement on the quality of life (*Ibid.*, p. 320). (3) Self-control—if an individual is not controllable by others or the individual himself and herself, that would be equal to reaching a lower level of life. Furthermore, if the condition cannot be rectified medically the individual ceases to be a person just as the fetus is not a person (*Ibid.*, p. 320). (4) A sense of time—If a person cannot have the consciousness of the passage of time, he has ceased to be human (*Ibid.*, p. 320). (5) Sense of futurity—Fletcher argues that nobody can be further if he is unable to realize the futurity or that is yet to come. His argument is that sub-human animals do not look forward in time (*Ibid.*, p. 321). (6) A sense of the past—The memory or the consciousness to recall is a criterion for humanness (*Ibid.*, p. 321). (7) A capacity to relate to others—"Inter-personal relationships of the sexual, romantic and friendship kind, one of the greatest importance for the fullness of what we idealize as being truly personal", opines Fletcher (*Ibid.*, p. 321). (8) Concern for others—The concern and care for others is part of the criteria for humanness (*Ibid.*, p. 321). (9) Communication—"Utter alienation or disconnection from others, if it is irreparable, is dehumanization" (*Ibid.*, p. 322). This is related, says Fletcher, to the patients who won't hear, speak, feel or see others. (10) Control of existence—Invincible ignorance and complete helplessness is, according to Fletcher, opposite to humanness. A man lacks control can't be responsible and an irresponsible is to be sub-personal (*Ibid.*, p. 322). (11) Change and changeability—Fletcher states that to the extent that, if an individual is unchangeable or beyond any change, he denies the creativity of personal beings. It includes the change of condition and mind (*Ibid.*, p. 322). (12) Balance of rationality and feeling—The wholesome person will have rationality and feeling (*Ibid*, p. 323). (13) Idiosyncrasy—The identity and to be recognizable and callable by name is the characteristic of a person, says Fletcher (*Ibid.*, p. 323). (14) Curiosity—"To be without effect, sunk in anomie, is to be not a person. Indifference is inhuman (*Ibid.*, p. 322). (15) Neo-cortical function—For Fletcher this is the cardinal indicator of humanhood. If the cerebral is not synthesizing, that person is not human. The brain death is an example for this. In his view brain death makes anyone non-person, though the body remains alive (*Ibid.*, p. 323).

Joseph Fletcher provides some negative criteria too. (1) Man is not anti-artificial, since the test-tube baby can be artificial, but human. (2) Man is not necessarily parental since the nuns and monks can be human. (3) Man is not sexual essentially. (4) Man is not a bundle of rights. (5) Man is not a worshipper, since faith in supernatural realities is a personal decision. Like sexuality, it is not essential but only a fullness for him (*Ibid.*, p. 324).

Fletcher's understanding of value of person is questionable. He used these criteria to justify abortion, feticide and euthanasia. He does not regard all who are born and yet to be born as human beings. Those who are born with neo-cortical dysfunctions and those who has neo-cortical defects by some accidents or illness are also not human for Fletcher. Fletcher's concept of dignity of life is integrally related to the neo-cortical function. Those who are falling short of requirements laid by Fletcher are sub-human for him. So all 'human beings' are not human, for him.

The perspective on abortion and euthanasia are also the outcome of his relative understanding of humanhood and dignity of life. In the case of Arizona lady (she thought that she might bear a defective baby because she had taken thalidomide). Fletcher affirmed that even if the embryo was not deformed the decision would have been right (Fletcher, *Situation*, p.136). He also suggests pre-emptive abortion for the defective foetus. He neglects the concept of dignity of life which is a concern of Christian scripture and Jesus Christ. He emphasizes the quality of life which curb the birth of the deformed or genetically defective children (Joseph Fletcher, "Medicine, Morals and Religion" [*Theology Today* Vol. XXXI, No.1 (April, 1974), p.42; Hereafter Fletcher, "Medicine, Morals and Religion"]. It also suggests the termination of life in the cases of extremely severe condition.

In the case of euthanasia, he argues for administrating euthanasia if a person is medically pronounced as beyond recovery. For Fletcher, in the case of extreme illness, euthanasia is other—regarding act (Fletcher, *Morals* and *Medicine*, p. 191). In the extreme cases, he argues that a human being becomes a 'vegetable' and his humanhood is lost. For him, the incurable acute illness disintegrates the personality [Joseph Fletcher, "Our Right to die" *Theology Today*, Vol. VIII (May, 1991), p.203]. He feels the comatose is a meaningless life. So also extreme condition of pain and suffering.

Though he rejects the humanhood and dignity and dignity of the person who are under extreme sickness, he holds that patients are persons and not just bodies (Fletcher, "Medicine, Morals and

Religion", p.46). Though he does not provide much freedom in the case of acute sickness and the practice of euthanasia, he argues for freedom of choice in the case of patient's right to know the truth (Fletcher, *Morals* and *Medicine*, p. 35). Fletcher argues that in all situations the physician should tell the truth to the patient. Fletcher is situational all the time. It is doubtful whether it is wise to tell about the decisions of the physicians to the patients, and to inform the truth about the disease to the patient all the time.

Stewardship

Fletcher's concept of stewardship has no unified form. He dares to follow the situational position in this issue also. It is interesting to note that though he emphasizes that land is the gift from God [Joseph Fletcher, Ed. *Christianity and Property* (Philadelphia: The West Minster Press, 1947), p. 184. Hereafter Fletcher, *Christianity*] and God is the owner of the land and we are only stewards, he does not stress that life is fully controlled by God.

It is appropriate, first of all, to discuss his perspective on property in this regard. According to Fletcher, the modern free-enterprise theory recognizes land, capital and labour as the three important factors of property (Fletcher, *Christianity*, p. 176). He condemns the manipulation of property for power. In his theological and ethical outlook, he admonishes the share manipulation, holding of land out of use in order to charge higher price for it and promotion of artificial scarcity. These are all sinning for Fletcher (*Ibid.*, p. 181). For him ownership is contingent and not absolute, and we are just stewards. This is rightly understood by him from the Old Testament.

For him, God is the original owner of the land since he is the creator. He argues that we are not our stewards, but we are God's stewards to distribute his wealth to his family on earth (*Ibid.*, p. 191). The crucial task of stewardship, he opines, is to close the gap of private opulence and public poverty. He opposes any kind of manipulation in the production in order to exploit the people. He understands the humanity as a family.

He failed to realize that God has only absolute power over human life. He disallows the fact that human beings have no right to take one's own life. His understanding of abortion, humanhood and euthanasia prove that we are not stewards of our life, but we have absolute freedom over ourselves which is an existential view. His concept of stewardship is truncated since he does not give much importance to the right to live in all conditions of life.

Conclusion

Several points can be inferred from the ethical thought of Joseph Fletcher. It is very clear that he is being influenced heavily by the existentialism, utilitarianism and cultural relativism. His concept of love which is the key to his ethical approach. He is for situational decisions which is totally against any *a priori* rules. He does not have any respect for the natural law, which is legalistic. He is act-utilitarian. He is very relativistic. His situationism can be equated to relativism. This relativism is evident even in his concept of sexuality and marriage. Fletcher is quite personalistic.

His flexibility is seen even in the reproduction and birth control. He loose concept of sex and reproduction challenges the whole idea of sanctity of marriage. He has brought the scientific and technological manipulations into the arena of married life, which makes the covenant and fidelity in marriage stituational and unimportant. He failed to give importance to normative dimension of ethics.

The respect for life is disregarded by Fletcher. The idea of humanhood which is based on neo-cortical functions is to be challenged. Human beings are subjected to several forms of deformities by accidence or by birth which do not negate the humanhood and value of life. The image of God in human beings is disproved by him. His concept of stewardship is also inconsistent. Joseph Fletcher is very situational in his ethical approach. He is relativistic and personalistic.

8

Ethical Teaching of Religious Traditions

'Rita' is a common Indian term denotes the order and harmony. It opposes the chaos. It stands for what is good, right and true. The values can have a sequence as *artha, kama, dharma* and *moksha*. *Artha* means the goal of achieving prosperity, profit and wealth. *Artha* means economic and political aspects of man in society for Kautilya. *Kama* means the fulfilment of desires. According to Thomas Kadankavil, *kama* is a comprehensive term which includes all desires—desires ranging from the cravings of the flesh to the yearning of the spirit. *Kama* also helps to achieve the three *purusharthas*—wealth, righteousness and self-realization. *Dharma* holds or sustains duty, right and justice. There is *Sanatana Dharma*, *Svadharma* and *Kuladharma*. The *Varnashrama Dharma* which causes the caste discrimination is to be challenged. *Moksha* is the self-realization.

Sanadhana dharma means the teaching which is universally applicable. *Dharma* means that which holds together. *Karuna* is quite related to Christian understanding of Agape, so also *Ahimsa* to non-violence as they are rooted in the Christian principle of love.

Hinduism upholds *Karuna* and *Ahimsa*. It promotes the non-violence, welfare and protection of others. *Nishkamakarma* is doing a good *karma* without seeking any reward. The concept of '*thyaga*' or renunciation is another important idea. *Varnashrama dharma* is a value that comes from Hinduism which advocate the pollution. There are good elements and also contradictions like caste system in Hinduism. It talks about harmony or *Shanti* and respecting the mother earth. In the ecological point of view these are very important. We have to preserve the creation. Hinduism holds divergent values and ideologies.

The Advaita is for transcending the world. In the Vedic tradition there is consciousness of sin and evil which urges to seek forgiveness. The sacrifices and other rituals were conducted to overcome the personal sin. In the Upanishadic view, what is evil is *maya*, one has to overcome *maya* through *Jnana* or *Vidya*. Evil is understood as *Ajnana* or *Avidya*. The Upanishads affirm compassion, *ahimsa* (non-violence/do not harm) and truthfulness. The Advaita advocates amoral.

The Manusmrithi upholds the *Varnashrama Dharma*. The caste hierarchy and the caste discrimination are upheld by it. This legal literature also asserts the gender discrimination. It is quite patriarchal. The freedom of women is curbed. The rights and dignity of *shudras* and women were not accepted. The *dalits* had no right to property and religious rights (denied the purificatory rite).

The Epics, *Ramayana* and *Mahabharata*, portray the ideal men and women. They have also maintained the caste system. Women are discriminated. Women were idealized to make them idols. Sita was eulogized, at the same time the element of patriarchy is found in the epics. Women were objectified. *Bhagavad Gita* proposes the *Nishkama karma* (do the duty without expecting the reward). If everybody does so, including the high castes, it is a good idea. But it can be used as principle by dominant class to oppress the *Sudras* for their selfish motives.

In Jainism according to Dr. Radhakrishnan, the way to *Nirvana* for a person is by faith in Jina, knowledge of his doctrine and perfect conduct. It affirms right faith, right knowledge and right conduct. This is known as three jewels or '*triratna*'. There is also a fivefold conduct—(1) *Ahimsa*—positive kindness to all creation, (2) Charity and truth speaking, (3) Honourble conduct such as not stealing, (4) Chastity in word, thought and deed, (5) Renunciation of all worldly interests.

In the words of Dr. Radhakrishnan, Jaina ethics lay stress on both faith and works. To obtain merit one has to give food to the deserving, water to the thirsty, clothes to the poor, shelter to monks. The sins include *himsa*, untruthfulness, dishonesty, unchastity and covetousness, lack of self-control, defamation, abuse of others, hypocrisy and slander (*Indian Philosophy,* Vol. I, p. 327). Jainism questions the violence and it is a religion which upholds compassion, peace and non-egoism. It is against pleasure, possessions and selfishness.

Their concept is based on *Ahimsa* and *Thyaga* or non-attachment. Jainist philosophers say that in the immaterial and the material there is '*Jeeva*' so do not harm them. Life is to be protected and preserved. Jainism is non-egoistic. Selfishness is condemned. The whole consciousness should be sane (sanctity of life). A mendicant is not allowed to visit twice a house. It is to avoid any kind of attachment. Only deserted house or abandoned house he can choose to take rest. *Sanyasi* is totally detached. Having a non-attachment to the world, it is against the pleasure. '*Aparigraha*' is an important concept as it as against possessive nature and attitude.

Buddha and Mahavira are opposed to division of society into castes by virtue of birth (V.P. Jain "A Notion of Dharma in Jainism: A Comparative View" in *Glimpse of Jainism* edited by Sunder K. Jain, Delhi: Motilal Banarsidass, 1997, p.109). In Jainism *dharma* holds living things in happiness and lifts them up from worldly misery (*Ibid*., p. 114). It is the three-fold path of right faith, knowledge and conduct and it includes protection (non-violence) of all living things (*Ibid*., p. 114). Dharma is based on *samyaktva* which means right faith, right attitude and right view of life. It is also related to protection (non-violence) and non-attachment (*Ibid*., p. 115). Jainism also affirms the *Anekanta*, the principle of innumerable of views (recognizing various realities/ultimate) which appreciates or respects others' points of view. Jainism developed a non-ego centric, ecologically conscious and peace-loving ethical methodology.

Ashtangamarga and four noble paths are fundamental to Buddhism. The whole concept of Buddism is based on non-desire. Desire is the cause of all evils. We should avoid selfish desires. Buddhism upholds *karuna, ahimsa* and the dignity of all beings. Jainism and Buddhism emerged as protest against Vedic religion and Brahminism. *Ahimsa* is the key concept in both these traditions. For Buddha, suffering and pain is caused by desire, so it is important to detach from desire. It rejects the egoism or self-interests. Non-desire is the solution for suffering in Buddha's teaching. Jainism and Buddhism uphold the preservation of life, *ahimsa* and non-desire/pleasure which have ecological significance as the modern consumerist and industrial culture is very capitalistic in nature which is rooted in pleasure and profit so they do harm to the whole creation.

The eightfold path is very significant in Buddhist teaching: (1) Right beliefs, (2) Right aspirations, (3) Right speech, (4) Right conduct, (5) Right mode of livelihood, (6) Right effort, (7) Right mindedness, (8) Right rapture. Buddhism opposes sexual misconduct and evil deeds.

Jainism and Buddhism uphold *tyaga, karuna* and *ahimsa*. Buddhism emphasizes the charity, purity of conduct and resoluteness. According to Buddha, "From pleasure comes grief, from pleasure comes fear, he who is free from pleasure knows neither grief nor fear; he who, by causing pain to others, wishes to obtain pleasure for himself, he entangled in the bonds of hatred, will never be free from hatred" (*Dhammapada* 16.212; 21.291).

In Sikhism, God is *Satya* and is source of all goodness. True renunciation is giving up lust, anger, greed and falsehood. Sikhism is against caste discrimination and it prohibits smoking, alcohols and narcotics. It insists to get rid of the pleasures which are of the flesh. Sikhism repudiates anger and pride.

Zorastrianism (Parsi religion in India) emphasizes good thoughts, good works and deeds. Ethics is understood by them as the realisation of the divine attributes. To have a perfect ethical life imbibe, it suggests, wisdom, love, charity, honesty and industriousness in a person. God is the source of good.

In Islam, Allah is all compassionate, all benevolent and all determining. The fatalism (*kismat*) plays a crucial role in Islam. The teaching of Islam upholds the faith in Allah, the supreme. The Islam teaches to give alms/rewards (*zakat*) and show mercy to others. '*Sakat*' is the concept of sharing. The concept of *umma*—the community or brotherhood is important in Islam. God is compassionate, so God is Al-Rahim. Allah is the merciful. Polygamy was allowed only if one has a sound economic background to maintain more than one woman. A Muslim can marry more than one, if only he is able to deal fairly to all. Though the Triple *Talaq* was not permitted, it is widely used in Islam. According to Quran, "Those who swear off from their women, they must wait for four months" (2:226-235). The concept of Shariah, Muslim personal law, is related to *Talaq*. The *Jihad* or holy war is another crucial problem in Islam. They claim that it is to defend and not to offend. But *Jihad* is widely used by fundamentalists to threaten or to offend others.

The concept of agape, is the basis of Christian thought, so also the sermon on the mount. Just community or Kingdom of God is a just social order. It is God-centred socialism. Christianity upholds the welfare of all and the sharing of resources for the benefit of the poor. It urges to side with the marginated and work for their liberation from the clutches of oppression. It looks for a fair or egalitarian society. The Christian tradition emphasizes the wholeness or the holistic transformation. The spiritual regeneration and socio-political restoration and the affirmation of the dignity and rights of human persons are significant in Christian perspective. The Biblical vision upholds the dignity and rights of the subaltern.

The religion is to uphold love and justice. It is to work for the welfare of all and to maintain a harmonious society. Emancipating the oppressed, liberating the poor and upholding the human rights should be the vision religious traditions. The ethical teachings of the religions should guide the people to avoid the hatred and violence and to bring brotherhood and amity.

9

Bio Ethical Issues

Bio Ethical issues/Medical ethical issues are very crucial ones today. The genetic studies (e.g. genome) is emerging and it takes a rapid pace as the issues like cloning takes momentum. Bio ethics is concerned of the experimentation on human body by the use of modern science and technology.

1. Artificial Insemination/Invitro Fertilization (IVF)

There is homologous (Artificial Insemination by husband—AIH) heterologous (Artificial Insemination by Donor—AID), artificial inseminations and fertilization. This is done by injection of an amount of fluid. It is the introduction of the male sperm into female organism without normal intercourse. AIH is objectionable to some Christians, especially, to Catholic Church, since the sperm is collected by masturbation, which is considered as sinful. Both AID and AIH are also considered by Catholic Church as violation of marriage bond.

Today the Semen is preserved in sperm banks by means of cryogenic technology. In *In-vitro* Fertilization, ova and sperm are combined in a glass and transferred to mother's womb, when there is problem with fallopian tube or any other problem. It is test-tube baby. It is also possible to have surrogate mother (borrow a woman's womb) when it is not possible to deposit (combination of ova and sperm) it in mother's womb. She is only a carrier to give birth to a child. The first test-tube baby was born in July 25th, 1978, known as Louis Joy Brown in England. It is used as a device to overcome the infertility or childlessness. It brings happiness and satisfaction and fulfilment for some parents. It avoids their emotional strain.

The advantage is that it provides the possibility to overcome the childlessness. But the problem is raised whether it is permitted to have technological intervention in human marriage. Ovum is fertilized outside the mother's body and is implanted in mother's womb is certainly a manipulation. The use of third party sperm (AID) is certainly questionable, but it is difficult to challenge the AIH. The artificial Insemination by Husband should be accepted as a blessing to overcome infertility. According to James Gustafson, a scientist has no right to intervene in natural processes in such a way that he might alter what men believe to be, and value as the most distinctive human characteristics. He, further, states that a scientist has the right to intervene in the courses of human development in such a way that use of his knowledge foster growth in those distinctive qualities of life that humans value most highly and remove those qualities that are deleterious to what is valued.

The artificial insemination by the non husband donor will do no harm, if it is done by the consent of the spouse. In order to overcome the sterility and childlessness, the AIH can be used because there is no sexual intercourse with third party involved in it and the covenant fidelity is not broken because it is done with the consent of the spouse. To avoid the emotional strain and frustrations of partners, the decisions they take with mutual consent and trust have to be respected. Fletcher's idea is that God does not want anybody to be sterile. Any scientific method that is available can be used to overcome it. Ramsey allows artificial insemination by husband. Nobody can justify the AID for the sake of breeding progenies of superior quality. There are so many kinds of manipulations involved in AID.

This *in-vitro* fertilization may, in certain cases, transcend the sphere of parenthood. It can be reduced to research and experimentation alone. It also can be highly commercialized. It should be permitted only when the partners like to overcome sterility or the oviduct blockage of women. Further more, it has to be done only when all other possibilities are not successful. Ramsey's warning about the risk of producing severely defective infants as a result of invitro fertilization must be taken seriously. Richard A.

McCormick observes that Ramsey rightly maintain that embryo transfer necessarily means producing at least some severely defective infants (Richard, McCormick, "*In-vitro* Fertilization" in *On Moral Medicine* edited by Stephen E. Lammers and Allen Verhey, p. 334). He is also unsparing in his condemnation of the manipulations. Fletcher is so relative so that he did not take seriously the manipulations involved in it, but he leaves it to the freedom of choice of the people involved.

2. Abortion

Abortion is a very significant issue from the Christian view of life. There are several irresponsible foeticides and abortions. People detect the gender and 'kill off' the female foetus. There are clinics run legally and illegally to do this procedure. It is also done in the guise of Medical Termination of Pregnancy (MTP).

Before discussing the methods of abortion it is important to know the development of human embryo. The egg and sperm to unite to give forty-six chromosomes. At 45th day, (the brain is in developing stage), One can get electroencephalographic waves from brain. At eighth week there is brain. At the 9th or 10th weeks thyroid and adrenal glands in function. At thirteen weeks, fingernails. Following are the methods of abortion.

Dilation and Curettage (D&C)

Abortion is carried out between the 7th and 12th week of pregnancy by this technique, the uterus is approached through the female sexual organ (Vagina). The cervix is stretched to permit the insertion of instruments. The surgeon scrapes the walls of the uterus, cutting the baby's body to pieces and scraping the placenta from its attachments on the uterine wall.

Suction Method

It is widely used in United States. A powerful suction tube is inserted through the open cervix. This tears apart the body of the developing baby and the placenta, sucking them into a jar. These smaller parts of the body are recognizable as arms, legs, head, etc.

Salt Poisoning/Salting Out

This method is carried out after sixteen weeks of pregnancy, when enough fluid has accumulated in the sac around the baby. A long needle is inserted through the mother's abdomen directly into the sac surrounding the baby and a solution of concentrated salt is injected into it. The baby 'breathes' in and swallows the salt and is poisoned by it. It kills the baby. The mother slowly goes to labour about a day later and delivers a dead, shrivelled baby.

Hysterotomy

If it is too late to use D&C, or any other method, then hysterotomy is used. It is same as caesarean. Hysterotomy is used to kill the baby.

Manual Vacuum Method

Manual vacuum aspiration (or mini-vac) is an abortion technique that is becoming widely available. In North America, it was widely used in the 1960s as a technique that could be used in the third world, because it does not need electricity. A hand held syringe creates a tiny, localized vacuum that removes embryo. The amount of cervical dilation is less than with a conventional abortion because of the smaller size of the instrument. It creates less discomfort and it is a simple and safe procedure that gynaecologists can use in their office without a general anaesthetic. This technique is limited to the interval from 3 to 6 weeks of gestation.

D&X Abortions

It is an abbreviation of 'Dilate and Extract'. The cervix is dilated. The foetus is delivered feet-first. Its brain is removed. This shrinks the foetal head, and kills the foetus. The procedure is done during the fifth month of gestation or later. The surgeon inserts a sharp object into the back of the foetus' head, removes it, and inserts a vacuum tube through which the brains are extracted. The head of the foetus contracts at this point and allows the foetus to be removed easily from the womb.

In the context of abortion, the foeticide is a very common and serious problem. Sex determination and the consequent abortions are widely prevalent. The female foeticide is done in a large number in the cities. It is a crime against humanity, especially to the woman Their dignity and right to live are being questioned. Though the exact number of foeticides are not known, it runs in thousands in every town and cities.

The pre-marital and extra-marital sex and also the aversion towards the girl child lead to foeticide. Recently a group of priests expressed their concern over the reduction in female membership suspect that it might be the result of female foeticide. The foeticide affects badly the health of person, and not only that, it will be a crime against humanity. Our former President Shri K.R. Narayanan has stated that the female one is not even safe in the most secure place. He was referring that even in the womb of mother, the foetus is not safe.

The issue is whether one can kill the foetus? The traditional concept 'do not harm' is applied by Catholics in this regard. They argue that no one has the right to take one's life. Life is given by God. It is a serious question whether one can abort the foetus which has genetic disorders, or the foetus which is formed by rape? Therapeutic abortions are widely used. If there are adequate reasons like grace genetical disorders, abortion can be found as responsible.

The abortion should not be practiced irresponsibly. It can be resorted to avoid birth because of incest or rape. The ill-health of the mother is another reason for abortion. Abortion should not be allowed for therapeutic reasons unless the foetus has a serious defect. The freedom of choice is important in the case of abortion and nobody should be coerced into it. Abortion should be the last resort. Hunter P. Mabry suggests that "abortion should be a last resort and not an automatic first response". Hunter P. Mabry "Abortion: Some Theological considerations" Bangalore Theological Forum, Vol. IX, No. 2 (July- December, 1977 p. 17).

It is not always rational to cling on to the arguments such as "thou shall not kill" and traditional 'sanctity of life'. Abortions can be selective. The reasonable and responsible abortions should not be rejected because it serves the welfare of the whole humanity. At the same time the freedom of personal choice is not to be misused.

Paul Ramsey's approach towards the issue of abortion is not sufficiently flexible to exercize the personal freedom. He depends on the natural law theory and the traditional 'respect for life'. He is unconcerned about the issues such as rape, incest and the serious deformity of the foetus. It is true that there is a relationship between the foetus and the born child as Ramsey argues. But whether a deformed foetus that has no possibility of becoming a fully developed human being should be born. Aborting such a foetus and preventing its birth into a baby to face a world full of misery for itself is not murder but an act of compassion. It depends on the nature of the case and our sense of responsibility.

3. Screening

Amniocentesis is a test that can be done on a pregnant woman to detect certain genetic defects in the unborn baby. This test also can determine the sex of the unborn child. Amniocentesis cannot be done before the 16th week of pregnancy and usually done between the 16th to 20th weeks. The process is that a long needle is inserted through the abdominal wall of the mother to be, through the uterus, and into the amniotic sac in which the developing baby is floating in the amniotic fluid.

A portion of the fluid is sampled and cultured. It is chromosomal study to trace the chromosomal abnormalities. Some parents chose this method to opt abortion if abnormality is detected. Actually, the amniocentesis was invented by Sir Arthur Lilley for the purpose of saving the life of an unborn baby with an Rh incompatibility disease. (Rh—Rhesus factor—Rh Baby is infant with hemolytic disorder from its blood being Rhesus-positive and mother's Rhesus-negative. Rhesus factor is the antigen occurring in red blood cells of most persons). The risk of amniocentesis includes the damaging of the baby, tearing the uterus, introducing infection or precipitating miscarriage.

Screening involves so many risks as Ramsey has argued. The possible risks to the mother are haemorrhage, infection and spontaneous abortion; to the child, dangers include death, damage or inflection. [Charles Birch and Paul Albrecht, eds. *Genetics and the Quality Control* (Oxford: Pergamon Press, 1975), pp. 86-87].

The screening and the consequent abortion can be abused by medical profession. Ramsey's warning on screening would pave the way to curb its misuse such as female foeticide after the determination of sex. But on the other hand, his extreme inflexibility cannot recognize the legitimate need of screening except in the case of intrauterine therapy of the unborn child. Fletcher's approach is so relative that it can be manipulated to abort the female foetus and the foetus with minor defects. Unfortunately, he is not providing any regulations to curb these manipulations. Screening and its consequences deserve most serious consideration.

4. Euthanasia/Mercy Killing

The word 'euthanasia' derives from Greek, which means 'good and honourable death'. It was used to express the kind of assistance of the physician to alleviate the suffering of the dying patient. It came to mean to terminate the life of a patient beyond hope of recovery. In the cases of 'irrecovery', 'incurability', comatose (unconscious state—vegetative survival), or acute suffering, life is referred as losing humanhood or meaningless suffering and the patients opt for euthanasia.

For the patient, euthanasia can be voluntary or involuntary. Voluntary euthanasia proposes that the choice be made when the patient is calm and that he retains the right to withdraw his request when crisis comes. It can be done by withholding life-supporting systems like pacemaker or oxygen tube. The involuntary euthanasia is when the patient is an unconscious state, the relatives may decide for him to administer euthanasia.

There is Direct Euthanasia, (Active euthanasia) by removing the life-supporting mechanism. It is a deliberate action to shorten or end life. In the indirect euthanasia (passive euthanasia/Anti-Dysthanasia), the drugs are administered in terminal illness to relieve pain, or to render the dying person unconscious in order that he might not suffer too much pain and mental anguish. But the treatment may hasten the death.

One of the basic problem behind the abortion and euthanasia is the right to life. In the Nazi regime (Germany) euthanasia was applied to eliminate the weak, old, handicapped and the terminally ill. It is based on the Spartan dictum, "survival of the fittest". The questions about right to life and sanctity of life come over here. Do the genetically defected have the right to live? Do we have the right to speed up the death of a person. If every person is created in the image of God, no one has the right to take or give up life.

The experience of utter meaninglessness, pain and suffering is a tragic one. But taking one's life in a sensitive issue. There is also possibility of abuse in the name of euthanasia.

The possibilities to misuse euthanasia also should be given due attention. Ramsey thinks that Fletcher gives the impression that euthanasia is a common thing. Of course, there is every possibility that the physician may resort to irresponsible use of it. But Fletcher clearly disapproves it. He advocates the use of euthanasia only in the acute cases, whereas Ramsey does not permit euthanasia under any situation at all. Fletcher's handling of the issue of euthanasia has the merit of making use of freedom and choice to opt for it, and Ramsey's concern has the merit to curb exploitation for selfish ends.

5. Cloning

Cloning is deriving from the Greek word 'klon' which means piece of wood. It is used as a means to create the genotype. From the information so far the cloning is successful in animals. The lambs and calves are born through cloning. It is an attempt to create carbon copies or Xerox copies. It is an asexual reproduction (without sexual union) accomplished by the removal of nucleus (enucleate) of an ovum and replacing it by the nucleus of an asexual cell (e.g. a skin cell). The resulting baby is expected to be genetically identical with the donor of the nucleus. This bio- technology is understood as the manipulation on human life.

(a) The personhood is a very important question. The person without parents can create irresponsibility and also it can bring psychological problems.
(b) It is a violation of God's plan of marriage which is heterosexual and children are to be product of the love within the marital sexual relationship.
(c) There is a possibility of manipulation as to create any number of men and women with certain selfish motives.

Cloning is a form of asexual reproduction which can do terrible harm to a whole humanity or race of people. It poses serious dangers to the parenthood, conjugal love and the covenant relationship, as has been clearly pointed out by Ramsey. Because of the high degree of manipulations involved, it is very difficult to see if there can be any justifiable cause of cloning at all. Here Fletcher's attempt to justify it situationally does not have much credibility. Justifiably, Fletcher is objecting to creating distorted human beings (dwarfs, legless people etc.) which would negatively. affect the whole humanity, but he does not deal sufficiently with the issue of parenthood and conjugal love. Ramsey's rejection of cloning is quite justifiable. According to Harris, for Ramsey, cloning is a fundamental assault on the human and personal element in parenthood. Charles E. Harris, "Love as the Basic Moral Principle in Paul Ramsey's Ethics", *Journal of Religious Ethics,* Vol. 4/2, (fall, 1976), p. 248). Therapeutic cloning provides life or health for one, at the expense of another, which also cannot be upheld.

The experiments like cloning should not be permitted. The scientific or bio-research may take any road with excitement disregarding the good of the humanity. The scientific experiments should not be allowed to distort the whole concept of parenthood and conjugal love which are God-ordained.

6. The Patient's Right to Know

The patient has the basic right to know. It is true that there are occasions that the temperament of the patient may be such that telling the bare truth might produce undesirable psychological consequences and in effect hinder effective treatment. The doctor has to brief the patient the whereabouts to disease and the treatment given. The doctor also has the duty of keep secrecy of the information about the patient. It is also important to tell the truth to patient or the relatives in certain serious situations where death is imminent or certain as the patient may be getting opportunity to prepare himself/herself to face the death. According to international code of medical ethics, a doctor owes to his patient absolute secrecy in all which he has confided to him or which he knows because of the confidence trusted to him.

The patient's consent is part of the partnership between the patient and the physician. Alexander Capron rightly said that, the partnership of physician-investigator and patient-subject is based on the mutual recognition that the subject, as human being, retains the authority to determine what will be done to himself and to receive on explanation of all proposed procedures from his professional collaborator (Alexander Capron, "Informed consent in Catastrophic Disease Research and Treatment" in *Ethical Issues in Modern Medicine* edited by Robert Hunt and John Arras, California: Mayfield Publishing Company, 1977, p. 255).

Telling the truth to patient is part of integrity, respect and fidelity between patient and the physician. It also will reduce the object-subject relationship between them. The physician as a responsible person should disclose the truth or information to the patients since the right to know the truth is the legitimate freedom of any man. The patient is not non-human to hide the truth from him. The physician should not lie but tell the truth. According M. Ashley and Kevin D. O'Rourke, in order to accomplish the obligations to serve the patient's health, the physicians have the responsibility to refrain from lying or giving misinformation (M. Ashley and Kevin D. O'Rourke, "Principles of Professional Communication" on Moral Medicine edited by Stephen E. Lammers & Allen Verhey, p. 530).

7. *Contraception/Sterilization*

The issue is whether there is something wrong in using birth control devices. Gandhiji was advocating for 'Rhythm method' to control birth. Today, the condoms, pills, spermicides and sterilization are widely used to curb birth. The Roman Catholic Church is against the birth control devices as they argue that these are against nature. Contraceptive is also a hindrance to 'one flesh' aspect in the sexual act, for them. In the context of population explosion, there is reason to use the birth control devices. The Paul VI made the following commands in his encyclical 'Humanae Vitae' ('*Human Life*' which was published on 28 July 1968).

(a) Human life is sanctified.
(b) The marital life has its own glory and value and it is a treasure.
(c) The irresponsible and selfish attitude to artificial means of birth control is wrong.
(d) The means to prevent the fruit of sexual intercourse that is used before or after the sexual act is not permissible.
(e) In order to know the greatness of marital life, it is important to have self-renunciation and discipline.

The artificial devices for birth control such as contraceptives and sterilization do not affect the life badly, but the pills have great side effects. It is also noted that the banned pills are used in Asian countries. In marital life the devices for birth control play a very significant role in the lovemaking. These are also to be used as there is therapeutic or eugenic reasons. It is also used in the context of AIDS in order to protect from the infection. The person can be guarded from the AIDS infected partner.

The contraception and sterilization can be misused by not fulfilling the obligation to propagate as Fletcher argues, but they also can be used as a part of Planned Parenthood. In order to have responsible families in the context of marriage partnership, contraception and sterilization are significant. While talking about contraception, Carl Braaten has opined, "A conscientious decision to postpone or discontinue having children, if it is not made out of selfishness, is no way minimizes the meaning of their marriage partnership" (Carl E. Braaten, *The Ethics of Conception and Contraception* U.S.A Board of Social Ministry Lutheran Church in America, 1967, p. 13).

In the context of planned parenthood, the parents want to control birth, so contraception and sterilization can be helpful means to achieve it. In the context of planned parenthood, it would certainly bring happiness. In the context of population explosion, financial crisis and the better care of the children, these means of planning parenthood are important. Fletcher's attitude is more helpful to take responsible decisions as required by the needs of the time than Ramsey's which permits contraception and sterilization only for eugenic reasons. The wise and responsible use of these means could bring happiness and welfare to the whole of humanity. Ramsey's approach, because of its severe restriction, can stifle conjugal love and satisfaction. Irresponsible sterilization must be rejected.

Bio-ethical issues can bring serious problems to humanity. The experimentation or the intervention of science and technology on human body can cause harm on human beings. There are positive elements that bio-technology brings so also negative effects. The technology can be inhuman and demonic as it is misused. The intervention of technology should be challenged if it goes against the programme of God. But at the same-time, the positive element of technology should be integrated for the well being of humanity.

10

Poverty, the Plight of the World

One of the worst enemy of humanity is the poverty. It is a fierce demon which makes the life of the people miserable. Millions of people on this earth are affected by the extreme poverty. Poverty is the fate of many in the context of prosperity. Many are dying everyday because of poverty. In the context of war, ethnic violence, communalism, population explosion and natural calamities the poverty would be increased.

WHAT IS POVERTY?

Poverty is the state where people live below the subsistence level. The food, shelter and the employment are essential for the dignified existence of man. In India, around 40 per cent of the population live below the poverty line. Most of them are going to bed without a meal or with a square meal. Poverty is the situation by which one is not having enough income to have sufficient food, shelter and to have education and health. It is reported that in every minutes 12 children, below 5 years of age, are dying because of starvation. According to Government reports 1999-2000, the percentage of people below poverty line in India is 26.10 per cent nationwide. But this could be more. There are 1300 million poor in the world.

Most of the poor live in ghettoes or slum, the most unhygienic conditions. The slums are ever increasing in the Indian context as the poor are migrating to the cities to seek food and employment. The slum symbolizes the massive poverty. It is estimated that around 25 per cent of the Indian population in slums. They have no possibility for a dignified existence (Godwin Shiri, *Our Slums: Mirror a Systemic Malady*, Bangalore: ATC, 1999. p. 1). In all cities 500 to 700 slums exist which reflects the gravity of the problem. The poor are struggling for 'Roti' (food), *'Naukari'* (employment) and *Makan* (shelter).

Poverty line is explained as follows. The minimum required consumption expenditure level of items such as food, clothing, shelter, transport and health-care, which meets the average per capita daily calorie requirement of 2400 calories in rural areas and 2100 calories in urban areas, along with a minimum of non-fool expenditure. In 1979, the Planning Commission's task force worked out the monetary equivalents of these 100 ms at Rs. 49.9 per capita per month in rural areas and Rs. 56.64 per capita per month in urban areas (*Manorama Year Book 2002*, Kottayam: *Malayala Manorama* 2002, p. 566).

It is found as explained that Poverty-line is defined in terms of the minimum number of calories (around 2400) required for a human being to live and do ordinary work. This does not include other subsistence requirements like housing, clothing, health and education (J. Murickan ed. *Poverty in India: Challenges and Responses*, Trivandrum: The Xavier Board of Higher Education in India, 1988, p. 41).

According to T.G. Godard, poverty is an insufficient supply of those things which are requisite for an individual to maintain himself and those dependents upon him in health and vigour. In the words of Gillin and Gillin, poverty is the condition in which a person, either because of inadequate income or unwise expenditures, does not maintain a scale of living high enough to provide for his physical and mental efficiency and to enable him and his natural depending to the standards of the society of which he is a member (K. Singh, *Problems of Sociology*, Lucknow: Prakashan Kendra, 1991, p. 289). For Malthus, growth of population is the cause of poverty, but Karl Marx observes that exploitation is the main source of poverty.

The population is increasing in each second. The world population has reached around 600 crores. India has crossed 100 crores. Thomas Robert Malthus (1766-1834) is considered as the father of population study. He was a minister of the church of England and Professor of History and Economics at Cambridge

University. According to him, the population is regulated by passion for sex. He suggested certain means to control population growth. The important one is the reduction of birth rate. This is done by (1) a total abstention of marriage, (2) a prudential postponement of marriage, and (3) a voluntary abstinence within marriage. He was advocating only voluntary abstinence by couples and no means of birth control. He also see the poverty, famine, pestilence, war and malnutrition as the ways in which there is increase of death rate to reduce population growth (Paul J. Koola, *Population and Manipulation*, Bangalore: A.T.C. Publications, 1979, pp, 10-11). His theory is based on his understanding on natural law.

The Structure of Poverty

The poverty is contributed by the structural problems. The unequal distribution of land or income generating resources and the unequal distribution of food and resources are some of the important causes for the poverty. The accumulation of wealth by few is found among the capitalistic structures. In the context of Globalization is modern times, the Multinational Corporations, Transnational Corporations, World Bank and International Monetary Fund are playing key roles to structural adjustment programme which is part of New Economic Policy and the Global cheap labour economy. Globalization promotes disintegration as it widens the gulf between rich and poor. It promotes foul symbols of victory-prosperity of few and entertained efficiency and competition. It promotes neo-colonialism so entertained exploitation and oppression. It negates the kingdom values—love, justice and shalom (well being of all).

The competition and efficiency are considered as important factors in the globalized context. Here the lion's share of the population are sidelined. They would be found powerless and away from the mainstream of the society. The exploitation, oppressions and different kinds of injustices contribute to poverty. Lack of fair wages and reduction in the employment opportunities also contribute to poverty. The free market economy badly affects the internal economic system of any country as it brings crises in the field of agriculture and industry. The product that is dumped by the foreign forces into the market damage domestic economy of countries, especially third world countries.

The Western colonialism had tapped the resources of third world countries and the left the people as poor. The neo-colonialism breaks down the domestic economy of third world countries by tricks and force. The Asian, Latin American and the African countries are much affected by the neo-colonialism. In order to make an economic crisis, the Westerners exported their goods to the third world market as part of free-trade. As a result the domestic industry, agriculture and cattle-rearing are adversely affected which also contributes to poverty. The Somalian famine and Rwandan crisis are created by the neo-colonial powers (Michel Chossudovsky, *The Globalization of Poverty*, New Delhi: Madhyam Books, 1977, pp. 76 ff; 101 ff; 111 ff).

Response to Poverty

In the context of extreme poverty, all religious traditions and secular ideologies should come together to help humanity to overcome this plight as care and concern should be shown to the marginated and poor. God is the friend of the poor (*Deenabandhu*). He hates violence (*himsa*) in the form of exploitation. Alleviation of poverty is the responsibility of each person as they should share and contribute to the welfare of the other.

The family planning is very important to control population growth. We are one, we have one is the slogan today. The nuclear families are being developed in place of extended families. There should be a control of birth rate. This is done, positively to take care of the welfare of the parents and children. The artificial means of birth control are suggested (contraception and sterilization) to regulate the population growth. There is a wide conscientization programme in this regard. It is important to note that the force should not be used in this matter. It should be a voluntary decision of the family.

The church should also teach the families for responsible parenthood and family planning. Control of birth is not sin. The human beings are given wisdom to act responsibly in the context. This can be applied in the situation of population explosion. Though food is entrusted by God for the need of the whole people, it is controlled by few, so there is no proper distribution. When there is no proper distribution and availability of food, it can led to malnutrition or death.

The population growth can also result in issue of space land and shelter. To an extend these issues are real. But it should be kept in mind that there is enough space for the people to survive if we avoid the vested interests. The possessive nature of man control vast amount of food, land and other assets for their own welfare or selfish interests. Though population growth may affect the issue of poverty, it should not be exaggerated. There are several other structural problems (e.g. Feudal system) that lead to poverty.

Right to food and shelter are the basic rights of human beings. M.M. Thomas, the theologian, has referred this as the right to bread. The 'anawim' (Hebrew word for poor) and 'Ptokos' (Greek word for poor) represent the widows, oppressed and the helpless ones. They depend on others for their survival. They also include the slaves, orphans and sojourners (Zc. 7:9-10; James 1:27; Lev. 19:10; Ex 22:21-22). They are the debtors and the landless. The Biblical insights uphold the sharing of resources, safeguarding the welfare of the poor and justice. It challenges the feudal structure that promote poverty (LK. 4:16-21; MK 12:41-44; LK 19:1-10; Amos 5:11; 5:5; 4:4-5).

The churches should unite to resolve the issues of poverty. Strategies and financial policies are to be developed to confront the situation of poverty. Sharing the resources, involving in rehabilitation and development, creating the employment opportunities, and protesting against the development of exploitative structures are important to deal with the issue of poverty. The rich held the lion's share of the resources which should be released for the benefit of the poor.

11

Economics and Eco-Ethics

The term ecology or oekologie was coined in 1866 by the German biologist Ernst Haeckel to describe the study of the relationship between living organisms and their environment (R.L. Sarkar, *The Bible, Ecology and Environment*, Delhi: ISPCK, 2000, p. 59). Ecology is derived from the Greek word 'oikos' means 'house' or inhabited world. It is referring to our earth. The earth constitutess the biotic (living) and abiotic (non-living) elements.

There is biodiversity, which is a boon to the whole earth and it has to be protected. Various species of animals and plants are 'killed of' to fulfil man's selfish interests. For collecting skin, hair or horns the animals are disturbed by human beings. For the sake of money or in the name of urbanization and development many valuable plants and trees are destroyed. Many animals and plants are facing exinction. They have the right to survive, and they are essential for the life of humanity.

About deep ecology R.L. Sarkar describes, the Norwegian philosopher Naeess first used the term in 1973. The concept of deep ecology uses the term 'ecosophy' which derives from the Greek 'Sophia', 'Wisdom', and 'eco'= house. It studies our place in the Earth Household and concerns itself with earth wisdom. It is inspired by the science of ecology and system theory. It draws on wider philosophical and religious traditions. The exponant's of deep ecology are said to 'deep' because they look to the fundamental principles which are at the root of our environmental crisis. Deep ecology goes beyond the so-called factual science level to the level of self and Earth Wisdom. It gives us a philosophical foundation for environmental activism. It has sound environmental ethics.

According to Naess, there are eight principles of deep ecology. Deep ecology seeks to challenge our culture's fundamental human assumptions, especially those which have led us to accept materialism, militarism, and human domination over nature as normal human behaviours. Deep ecology seeks to understand and challenge the root causes of our planetary despoliation. From the set of principles of Naess concept or deep ecology other deep ecologists have identified on a more precise platform, which specifies political values flowing from deep ecology: the primary of wilderness, a sense of place, opposition to stewardship, opposition to industrial society, spirituality, and self-realization:

1. The wellbeing and flourishing of human life on Earth have value in themselves (synonyms: intrinsic value, inherent value). These values are independent of the usefulness of the non-human world for human purpose.
2. Richness and diversity of life forms contribute to the realisation of these values and are also values in themselves
3. Humans have no right to reduce this richness and diversity except top satisfy vital needs.
4. Human flourishing of human life and cultures is compatible with a substantial decrease of the human population. The flourishing of non-human life requires such a decrease.
5. Present human interference with the non-human world is excessive and the situation is rapidly worsening.
6. Policies must therefore be changed. These policies affect basic economic, technological, and ideological structures. The resulting state of affairs will be deeply different from the present.
7. The ideological change is mainly that of appreciating life quality—dwelling in situation of inherent value—rather than adhering to an increasingly higher standard of living. There will be profound awareness of the difference between big and great.
8. Those who subscribe to the foregoing points have an obligation directly or indirectly to try to implement the necessary changes.

Social Ecology

The term social ecology was first used by the American ecologist, E.A. Gutkind in 1954. It describes that tendency within the green movement which sees the present ecological crisis as a result of the breakdown of the fabric of both society and nature. It is concerned with the green movement with democracy, community and co-operation. It has a realization that there exist social and political institutions of domination and hierarchy that block the liberation of nature and humanity.

Social ecologists believe in the ecological principles of unity in diversity. Social ecology sees balance and integrity of the ecosphere as an end in itself. It wants to create a dynamic social movement to transform the way we find our place within nature and to change our relationships with each other and the non-human world. Social ecologists challenge the fundamental premises of Western civilization.

The main concern of the social ecologists is to change society in order to change our relationship to nature. Deep ecologists lay stress on the direct relationship between the individual and nature unmediated by society. According to social ecologists the role of society is responsible for creating the ecological crisis; according to the deep ecologist, on the other hand, each citizen is responsible for the planet earth.

The social ecologists tend to be more humanist, the deep ecologists are more spirituality inclined. Social ecologists believe in participatory democracy; deep ecologists are influenced by eastern religions and western process metaphysics. Social ecologists have sympathy for the poor and the oppressed; the deep ecologists tend to retreat to the wildness and identify with tigers, bears, trees, valley, lakes and rocks (Bible Ecology and Environment, pp. 64-65).

Ecological issue is one of the most important issue today. It is the creation of the modern technology and industrialization. In the guise of development, the technology is used without considering the environment. The ecology and economics are quite related in this regard. For the sake of economical development the environment was mistreated. Fr. Samuel Rayan has aptly said: "It is modern technology and development ideology as understood and practised by a particular economic system, that have polluted the earth and led to the ecological crisis" [Samuel Rayan, "Theological perspectives on environmental crisis" *Religion and Society,* Vol. XXXVII. No.2 (June) 1990, pp. 19-20]. Dr. K. Rajaratnam also agrees with this understanding. He states, 'Environment and economics have indeed been living together for ages in all illicit and irresponsible relationship bringing forth their own offspring that are menace to society" (K. Rajarathnam, "Economic implications of environmental rights and privileges" in *Ecology and Development: Theological Perspectives* edited by Daniel D. Chetti, n.p.; UELCI/ GLTCRI/BTESSC, 1991, p. 1). Vandana Shiva also approves that there is a close connection between ecology and economics. The economic system contributes to ecological crisis. According to her, "The age of enlightenment, and the theory of progress to which it gave rise, was centred on the sacredness of two categories; modern scientific knowledge and economic development. Somewhere along the way, the unbridled pursuit for progress, guided by science and development, began to destroy life without any assessment of how fast and how much of the diversity of life on this planet is disappearing" (Shiva, Vandana, *Staying Alive: Women, Ecology and Survival in India*, New Delhi: Kali for women, 1988. p. XIV). This paper is an attempt to look at the causes of the ecological problems, the ethical responses, the tribal response and the challenges. It would be focusing on the relationship between the economics and ecology in the ecological issue.

The Main Causes for the Environmental Problems

Samuel Rayan is of the opinion that the toxic chemicals used excessively undermine health of animals, plants and man. This is one of the reasons for the present ecological crisis. The capitalist development models also invite the ecological problems. So Brindavan Moses arms these dehumanising developmental patterns. He opines, "any development which dehumanises people and brings about environmental degradation is anti-development. Therefore, the path and pace of development must be determined by the people living in that locality or region or in the social environment. [Brindavan C. Moses, "So called development, environmental degradation and people's struggle against them" *Religion and Society,* Vol. XXXVII, No. 2 (June) 1990, p. 80].

Man's selfishness which is the result of sinfulness is one of the main reasons for ecological crisis. The economics with wrong ethics has contributed much to this global dilemma. Telling about the human sin and its far reaching consequences John Carmody has said, "for example, the pollution of the ecosphere testifies to our sinfulness. The world has stood before us, ready to cooperate and serve, and we have turned much of the world into garbage. The injustice of the society also testifies to our sinfulness. Fellow human beings have stood alongside us, asking to be treated as we have made wars and rapacious economics, slaveries and torture cells" (John Carmody *Ecology and Religion*, New York: Paulist Press, 1983, p. 72). The air, water and soil is polluted very inhumanely by the modern society in the name of development. The survival of the living creatures is in real threat today. There is neither good water to drink nor fresh air to breath. It has become like S.T. Coleridge has portrayed in his poem "The Rime of the Ancient Mariner".

> Water, water, everywhere;
> and all the board did shrink.
> Water, water, everywhere;
> Nor any drop to drink.

According to Dleg Dreyer and Victor Los, "the prevention of the pollution of water is one of the most important among the ecological problems facing the developing regions" (Bells Los Dleg Dreyer and Victor Los, *Ecological Problems of Developing Countries,* Delhi: Ajanta Publications, 1989, p. 81). The resistance of man to different diseases is considerably reduced and the respiratory problems are increasing in a dangerous pace. The natural disaster like the earthquakes are also increasing because our environment is not given much attention.

The recent Narmada Valley Project and so many other projects like this sort have denied the rights of the aboriginals. Since ecology is related to man, animals, plants and whole system of nature, it should be given adequate care when we deal with them. The deforestation and evacuation of the homogeneous people is a great threat to their existence. It curtails their freedom to move and survive, and it denies their sources of resources. The water is the very life to them, since they depend much on it for cultivation, fishing and living. The rivers are divine for them. They adore rivers, since it provides life to them. If we pollute the rivers by chemical waste, it badly affects the life of the plants, animals and man. The polluted water is peril to cultivation too.

According to Atlar Chand, "economic progress and preservation must go hand in hand. We cannot have one without the other". It is important to note that the transnational corporations and other neo-colonial enterprises also are contributing to the violation of nature.

According to Atlar Chand : Being the main instrument of neo-colonialist exploitations, the transnational corporations (TNCs) are chiefly to blame for the emergence and worsening of environmental problems in the developing countries. INCs are also responsible for the plunder of natural resources and the degradation of the environment in the developing world. It is the operations of the TNCs in industry and agriculture that are having the greatest impact on the environment in the developing world (*Ibid*., p. 69).

The MNCs and TNCs follow the capitalist models of development and they are after making profit by any means. So this has necessitated the exploitation and it becomes a peril to water, Air, soil and even to the whole living and non-living beings. Reflecting on the ecological issue Klostermaier has said, "the ecological crisis in its present form is a new phenomenon: it has to do with the spread of industrialization, urbanization, over population and exploitation of the earth" [Klaus K. Klostermaier, "Bhakti, Ahimsa and Ecology" *In Journal of Dharma* Vol. XVI, No.3 (July September) 1991, p. 246]. J.K. Jonathan is of the opinion that, "land is mainly polluted by the disposal of solid waste and chemicals" (J.K. Jonathan, "environmental degradation owing to population explosion" *Environment awareness and wildlife conservation* complied by A.K. Ghosh *et al.,* Calcutta: Zoological Survey of India, 1989, p. 26).

Disturbing nature will have serious consequences. It reacts sharply to any injustice done to it. Atlar Chand states, Environment is a dynamic, complex and inter-connected system in which nay action in one part, affects the other and reflects the inter-dependence of living things and their relationship with land, air, soil, plant, animals and other abiotic factors which influence the growth and development of man. These different components of the environment keep on interacting with each other to maintain a natural balance known as "ecological balance" in nature (Atlar Chand, *Environment Pollution and Protection*, p. 88).

The environment should be given utmost importance in our whole thinking and activities. On the whole, it is understood that the irresponsibility of man is the main cause for the present severe ecological problems. Man becomes self-centred and is after mammon. The irresponsible anthropocentrism is a grave danger in this respect The shift from God-centredness to man-centredness has resulted in the exploitation, manipulation and injustice of man over nature.

The Ethical Response to the Environmental Problem

On the theology of nature based on Genesis Chapters 1 and 2, Samuel Rayan has said, "nature is something God calls into existence feel and lovingly. God is pleased with her, he admires and appreciates her; he sees she is good and lovely. She is God's beloved. Once the earth is there, she is taken into partnership with God". [Samuel Rayan, "Theological Perspectives on Environmental Crisis" in *Religion and Society,* Vol. XXXVII, No. 2 (June) 1990. p. 26]. Nature is God's creation and it has to be well maintain. Man is not to dominate, but to serve the nature. Rayan states, "Allan Boesak observes that the Hebrew world translated 'to dominate' could be rendered to 'serve'. It is to serve the earth that man is commissioned". (*Ibid.,* p. 27). The fellowship or companionship between man and other creatures is significant. It should be kind of inter-dependent relationship rather than of domination.

According to Rudolf Heredias, human beings, then, are necessarily made companionship, for relationship with each other and all creatures, in a covenant, that like humans themselves, is an image of God's own covenant with people and this creation [Rudolf C. Heredias, "Towards an ecological consciousness Religious, ethical and spiritual perspective" *Vidyajyothi Journal of Reflection*, Vol. LV, No. 9 (September), 1991, p. 500].

While reflecting on Psalm 19:1, Thomas Sieger Derr has said: "Although nature is not divine, it has value nonetheless. This value is derivative from the fact of creation "God saw that it was good" when he created the natural world" (Thomas Sieger Derr. *Ecology and Human Liberation*, n.p.A WSCF Book, 1973, p. 12). A right attitude to economy or an ecology based economy is needed, since ecology and economy are inter-related. According to Derr, "the Steward is the house manager, "Oikonomos" the root word of both 'economy' and 'ecology'" (*Ibid.*, p. 72).

God has sole authority over the creation, so human beings cannot do any harm against creation. The arms race has done so much injustice to the nature. The Gulf War has spoilt the air and water severely. The oil slick has killed so many sea birds and other creatures. John Carmody states that "most universally, the current arms race and engines of ecological pollution are the most violent threats to the earth's survival" (Johm Carmody, *Ecology and Religion*, p. 154). He continued to say that:

> Since we did not make material creation, we do not have the right to destroy material creation. At best God placed nature subject to our responsible Stewardship. When we escalate the chances for nuclear war, expose the seas to widespread oil spillage, or countenance the rapid development of wildness areas and jungles, we fail a God-given trust. Nature does not exist simply for our if we speak from the perspective of the human rights, the right to live is not only the privilege of man, but also the right of whole creation.

In the opinion of John Carmody :

> "The mystery of nature's King, the Christology of nature's intelligibility, the occurrence of nature in God, and nature's impersonal revelations of God all argue that nature has right to be, a right to live, and a right to flourish apart from is utilities to human beings" (*Ibid*., p. 133).

The earth is understood as the Mother-Earth and she should not be discomforted. Sudhakar Ramteke made the following reflection on the title 'Earth-Mother':

> Without you everything would collapse and everything would be disintegrated. In fact, without you this universe will be broken into pieces. (Sudhakar Ramteke, Our good neighbours, *Reflections on Nature Environment and Ecology*, Delhi: Naudin Prakashan Kendra, 1989, p. 35).

The protection of nature or the conservation is very much evident in Indian culture, says Atlar Chand. In his opinion, in India environmental conservation is an old concept. Protection and preservation of life in all forms is deeply indebted in Indian-culture. The ancient Vedas as well as other scriptures have specific reference on protection of nature and interdependence of all forms of life—plant, animal and human. Indeed, the interdependence of life forms and their mutual co-existence constitute the essence of Indian vision and provide the foundation of the philosophy of non-violence (Anand Veeraj, "Eco spirituality and the religious community" *Indian Theology Today*, Vol. XLVIII, No.2 (July) 1991, p. 141].

Various theological thinkers today have developed an ecospirituality. A spirituality which undermines ecological concerns is invalid and inadequate. Anand Veeraj says:

> Rights to existence and self-realization for every species, whether sentiment of non-sentiment are recognized and upheld. Ecological democracy is advocated and supported within the community of nature. For eco-spirituality valid and authentic spirituality is that which recognizes the

egalitarian rights of the divine, humans and nature, making a democratic community (Atlar Chand, *Environmental Pollution and Protection*, p. 30).

Walter Gaslick has described the spirituality as follows when he talked about ecological spirituality:

> Spirituality is that dimension of inner life that is attuned to the things that are understood to be most valuable in life; it motivates and guides significant activity. An ecological spirituality, then, is attuned to the worth of the nexus of nature. [Walter B. Gaslick, "The Bible and Ecological Spirituality" *Theology Today*, Vol. XLVIII, No.2 (July) 1991, p. 185].

He proposes four components to an ecological spirituality. It is worth looking:

1. A recognition of the interconnectedness and interdependence of things in the natural world is crucial.
2. Sensitivity of ecological interconnectedness leads to the recognition of the gracility of most environmental system. The 'ecological spirituality will include a commitment to protect the natural world'. He states again that 'theologically, it seeks our covenational protection of God's created order'
3. The commitment to protect the natural environmental must be grounded in an appreciate affirmation of the richness of the web of life and indeed the grandeur of the whole cosmos. The appreciation arises out of experiences of the capacity of nature to speak to human in ways that evoke wonder, elicit awe, and generate self-imposed restraint'. (*Ibid*., p. 186)
4. 'No ecological spirituality will be complete without a resolve that issues in actions on behalf of those aspects of the natural world that one must appreciate. Not only in ecological understanding and appreciation of nation is required; one must have the power actively to live up to one's moral commitments to protect the environment (*Ibid*. p. 187).

The eco-spirituality affirms the value of life since life is from God. Bible does not deny the preservation of life. The Christian spirituality has to accept single-mindedly the value of life as we found in Jainism and Buddhism. We are not supposed to do harm to our fellow human beings. This is portrayed by Jesus through his very words, "Love your neighbour as thyself" (Luk. 10:27) Bible looks forward a day when the whole creation co-exists harmoniously (Isa. 11:1-9).

It is quite important to look at the tribal response to the environmental problems. Nirmal Minzhas beautifully depicted the tribal attitude to creation as follows:

> The indigenous people all over the world, including those in India affirm, 'land is life'. No land no life. Land here means the land one lives on now, the trees and plants he relates himself with day and night, and even the whole earth (Nirmal Minzhas, "Primal Religious Perspectives on Ecology", *Ecology and Development*, edited by Daniel D. Chetty, p. 50).

The tribal people are the supreme example for ecological concern. The animals, plants and the human beings are quite interdependent in their thinking. According to Sanjay Basu Mallick, "Indigenous people always try to tame animals and develop a human relationship with them. They practice hunting only during a certain season of the year. Their sense of keeping balance of ecology is amazing" [Sanjay Basu Mallik, "the Integrity of the Variegated Creation", *Religion and Society*, Vol. XXXVII, No. 2 (July) 1990, p. 85].

According to Wati Longchar, the earth is divine for the trials, so the earth and God are interrelated. He says:

> Different versions of our creation stories tell us that the earth and everything in it is God. To destroy this earth means to destroy God. The earth is divine. Hence, people called the earth as the Mother God and regarded as sacred.

> It is through this Mother God that all the existence of all life is made possible.

He also observes that "the tribal religion affirms that God made everything good in the beginning". (*Ibid.*, p. 19). This thought is integrally related to Biblical thinking. According to him, the tribal religion is also a challenge to sanctity of life and integral oneness of nature and divine. He states, "the concept of the sanctity of life and oneness with nature and divine is the basic affirmation of tribal religion" (*Ibid.*, p. 21).

The Challenges Ahead

In a world of acute ecological crisis, it is quite crucial for man to be a responsible being. The false motives of man is primarily responsible for this pathetic condition so he has to take utmost care to preserve the creation. The 'Capitalist based and consumer-oriented societies', (Eric J. Lott, "An Eco-theology for the future resources from India's past, Adventurous Faith Transforming Vision edited by Arvind P. Nirmal, Madras. GLTRCI, n.d. p. 29) have to be demolished. Our development models should be radically shifted and I have to be made ecologically oriented.

The Gandhian idea of development is quite concerned of the ecology. It is against the rash industrialisation and exploitation of natural resources. Gandhiji's idea of development is rooted in conservation. This should be given adequate attention in this respect. Dr. Rajarathnam's comment is quite relevant at this point. He states, when foreign experts discover Mahatma Gandhi, his economics and his methodology most relevant, perhaps the only relevant model to salvage the world from the brink of its ecological disaster. Indian economists and scientists are still shy to turn to Gandhi. (K. Rajaratham, "Economic Implications of Environment Right and Privileges", *Ecology and Development: Theological Perspectives* edited by Daniel D. Chetti, p. 13).

The church and other organizations should strive hard to conscientize the masses about the consequences of the ecological problem. This can induce them to work for creating the ecologically-oriented environment. The role of Baba Amte and Medha Patkar in Narmada Valley '*Andolan*' is quite admirable. An awareness should be created to protest against the disposal of chemical waste to the water, air and oil. We have to works also together for a nuclear-free world. The people from all religions and ideologies should work together for an ecologically oriented world. People have individual and collective responsibility to create an ecologically balanced world order. We should also develop an ecologically conscious economics in order to redeem ourselves from the ecological disaster.

12

An Ethical Response to War and Peace

Peace and harmony are the significant themes for the well being of the whole of humanity. We are to live and let live. God's intention is also to prevail shalom everywhere. The hatred, rivalry and the spirit of competition and domination should go. As against the plan of God, enemity and divisive elements are springing up. The rivalry at last ends up in unhealthy competition, the war. War is the ultimate form of cruelty against the other.

The world had witnessed two great world wars and their atrocities. The worst of their consequence was the bombing of Hiroshima and Nagasaki (both in Japan) in the Second World War. The people of the country of Japan are still suffering from that terrible act of United States and its allies. The former president of America George Bush had confessed that it was an act of terror. He apologized for it. Anyone can apologize after any insensible, irresponsible and immature and deliberate inhuman act. The bombs that were dropped at Hiroshima and Nagasaki were Atom bombs. Now, there are more terrible Nuclear Weapons. So it is very important to dwell upon this issue of arm-race.

Science and Technology are originally meant for the total progress of humanity. They are to be used to improve the quality of life of mankind. Unfortunately, these are used to annihilate the weak. When two countries are equally good in their Military Power they never go for testing their strength because of the sheer fear. If some countries are found to be weak, the powerful ones try to attack them. This is what exactly super powers and its allied countries doing today. If we recall the gulf war (Iraq *vs*. US and allies), We will realize that what US and its gang done was totally reprehensible. Instead of going for a ground battle (using Naval support and air covering), they had bombarded the cities and have caused severe harm to the common people. The innocent people including women and babies were killed. Women and children are usually the victims of war, communal riots or any disturbances of this sort. The wars have become a fight between common people and soldiers rather than between soldiers and soldiers. Indiscriminate kind of wars have made the life of humanity miserable. In the present War (2004) between Iraq and US allies, Iraq was destroyed by bombing without a real cause.

Atomic power has been used for many years in warfare. The nuclear weapons kill thousands in seconds through the bomb blast and other explosive elements. Japan is suffering the consequence of the American bombing in the Second World War. The radioactive elements are affecting badly even the newly born children, which brings genetic disorders. All nuclear powers are conducting the nuclear tests which ever pollute the atmosphere and wipe out thousands of living organisms which upholds the ecological equilibrium. The explosion and the radioactive elements do harm to the life of the plants, animals and human beings.

The biological weapons are said to be more dangerous than chemical and nuclear weapons. The chemicals or toxic elements are used in the chemical war which kills when one inhales the toxic chemical substance. It is the severe threat to the existence of humanity. The Bio-weapons are a threat to humanity. It is observed that biological weapons are easy to make and easily available.

The most potential bio-weapons category includes the anthrax, plague, Tularaemia, small pox, and Ebola-influenza hybrid. These bacterias can inflict heavy tolls. The terrorist are using these weapons against their enemies in-order to offend them. In the Afghan-US War (2001-2002), the anthrax was used by Afgan-centred terrorists. The innocents will also be affected by the use of bio-weapons.

War is a crime against humanity. It should not be promoted. Those who involve in war and other innocents will be adversely affected by war. It is a waste of money. It creates ecological disaster and the whole creation will be affected by war. Pollution of air, loss of life and famine and pestilence are the consequence of war, so war is inhuman.

The amount of money used for Nuclear and other kinds of sophisticated weapons are unpardonably high. Instead of bringing happiness, peace and life, money is used to buy weapons to cause misery, famine, disease and death. More people and countries are fabricating strategies to exploit and to cause harm to others rather than bringing up life and welfare for the humanity. While there are crucial problems like poverty, malnutrition, epidemics, unemployment and injustices, it is quite unfortunate that our priorities are set on arm-struggle and cold war. Wars have made the life of human beings miserable, and people are between the struggle of life and death. The words of the tireless apostle of lepers Raoul Follereau are very significant to be recalled. He said: "Just give me the money for a single atomic bomber, and I will care the fifteen million lepers on this planet" (Quoted in *Beyond Love* by Dominique Lapierre, p. 36).

The war between the rival factions in different countries are the most horrible ones today. Wars are making this world a hell. The common people are moving to different places for security reasons. They have to run for life. Wars begin in human hearts, told Leo Tolstoy. This is a true statement. Wars are fought to conquer and to take revenge. So war is antithetical to peace. It is ridiculous to combine a slogan like 'war is for peace'. Violence, indeed, will breed violence, and it will bring more misery to humanity. 'War is for destruction'. War will not resolve any problems, since it promotes hatred and rivalry. Charles Curran, the American moral theologian, recognized the great need and importance of peace for good of all human beings. For him, the use of nuclear weapons is totally wrong, and the just war theory is a deception. He suggests that violence or force can be used only against the bearers of force. For him, the whole Christian message is to achieve peace and justice in the society (*Ongoing Revision in Moral Theology*, pp. 165-72). The Indian religious traditions also have given utmost importance to the principles 'do not harm' and '*Shanti*'. Buddhism and Jainism have been the greatest challenge in this regard. Both these religious tenets uphold the principle of non-violence. Hinduism also later on tried to accommodate this principle.

The whole Christian message is of love, peace and compassion (Mathew 5:38-44). Buddha also hails compassion. He said, "only virtue gives a good *Karma* and the greatest of all virtues is compassion".

If we are not moved by the love and compassion, the world would be doomed by the terrors of war, strife and riots. The brotherhood of mankind has to be accepted by all in order to overcome the enemity. 'Shalom' should be the catchword and not war. While war is destructive '*Shanti*' is creative. Upholding '*Shanti*' is the need of the time.

13

Ethics and Subaltern Perspectives

Antonio Gramsci used the term 'subaltern' to refer to the marginated ones. The marginated ones are powerless and unorganized groups who are economically poor. The subaltern are the 'slaves' and the dependents. They are exploited and oppressed by the 'powerful'.

The subaltern are socially alienated, economically poor and politically powerless. They are away from the main stream of the society. Their dignity and rights are denied. They include the labour class, the victimized women, the tribals, the blacks and dalits. The subaltern are the 'last' and the 'least'.

The poor is mainly an economic category. The poor are found among all groups of people. In Marxian view, the proletariat constitute the subaltern, but there is no reference to any particular group of people. It is a class distinction than racial, social or gender distinctions.

The centuries long oppressions and acute sufferings had been undergone by certain groups of people and they can be referred as the subaltern. The blacks and the dalits are racially discriminated. The tribals are the aboriginals and they wrongly are referred as 'uncivilized', 'uncultured' or 'savage'. They found forests as their habitat. The women who are victimized are also subaltern as they are oppressed in many ways (e. g. Sexually and socio-politically). The condition of the *dalit*, black and tribal women are so pathetic.

The Blacks and Their Plight

Colonialism and slavery had made the blacks the powerless. Africa was colonized and the whites had ruled them before they gain independence. Around six hundred years of colonialism has considered Africans as brutes. The Europeans had even sold them as slaves. They were employed in different countries to serve their purpose. The slave trade was common in United States of America even in the 19th century A.D. The Afro-Americans or U.S. minorities has suffered a lot. They had the similar experience like the *dalits* of India. The blacks were not permitted to enter into the hotels and buses. There was reserved seats for whites and blacks. It was quite discriminatory and inhuman. Their opportunities were curtailed. They lived in the ghettoes. Martin Luther King Jr. had organized the blacks and even dared to boycott buses which made the authorities to rethink their attitude to the blacks. Through the civil rights movement of 1960s the American blacks attained the political power which leads to their participation in the government and also to liberate themselves from the mistreatment or discrimination.

The rights of the blacks are questioned by the whites. The right to have a dignified life was denied. The civil rights movement had created conflicts, though non-violence was emphasized, which ultimately led to the affirmation of the rights of the blacks. They had the faith which coupled with hope that inspired them to sing 'we shall overcome someday'. Their faith was dynamic and hopeful about a bright future and these end up in the liberation of the blacks.

The Dalits

'Dal' in Hebrew and Sanskrit means 'scattered', 'crushed', 'oppressed', 'down trodden' or torn. The Adi Dravidas are the original inhabitants of India. Then came the Dravidians, who joined with Adi Dravidas and occupied the land of India. The Indus valley civilization was the contribution of Dravidians. They were the worshippers of Pasupati or Siva.

The Aryans were the latecomers in the history of India. They came with a crusading spirit and fought with Dravidians. They developed the *varna* theory and tried to subjugate the Dravidians. In the struggle, the Dravidians are divided into two groups. One group fled to the forests and hills to wage guerilla warfare against Aryans and they became tribals. Another group accepted defeat and went to the south who became the *dalits*.

The *dalits* are psychologically, physically, socially, economically, politically and religiously oppressed by the caste Hindus. The Aryan fascism dehumanized the Dravidians and the *dalits* are forced to do mean jobs, suppressed their voice and used violence over them. They are the alienated as their dignity and rights are denied. They are the landless and the poor.

The Hindu religious system legitimized the caste duty and the consequent oppressions over *dalits*. The *Kuladharma* (caste duty) is insisted on persons by birth. The social mobility is curtailed. The untouchability is legally curbed, but still it is prevalent in many contexts. The Ranvira Sena is involved in attacking the *dalits*. The *dalits* are even mercilessly burnt by the dominant caste. The *dalit* women were forced to walk naked through the streets. It is easy for the dominant to oppress the powerless dalits. The *dalits* are mostly belonging to the labour class. They are agricultural labourers or they work in unorganized sector. They are lowly paid.

The caste system is a centuries long evil in the Indian society. It is like the racial discrimination of the whites against the blacks. The Aryans are not willing to accept the dignity and rights of the Dravidians.

The Aryan scriptures also affirm the caste system. The Vedas, Upanishads, *Mahabharata* and the *Manusmriti* accept the caste hierarchy which is a dehumanizing principle. The de-legitimation of the sources are important to get rid of the prejudices against the *dalits*, and it can be done by re-reading the Aryan religious texts.

Bible is against the social evils. It affirms the rights and dignity of all human beings (Gen. 1:27,28; Acts 10). God does not tolerate the unfair relationship and the discrimination. God is just and righteous and he is for forming a society in line with justice. God sides the oppressed and he liberates them from the clutches of the dominant class. The marginated are taken care by God.

The Tribals

The tribals are a homogeneous group, which occupies a territorial limit, having a particular (or common) origin or ethnicity, customs beliefs and behaviour. The dominant groups categorises the tribals as 'no people', landless, powerless or 'uncivilized'. They are the savages in the understanding of the modern man. They live in the forests and very close to nature. They are the original inhabitants or aboriginals of the land. They are called as '*Adivasis*', '*Vanavasis*' or '*Kananavasis*'.

The dominant class tried their level best to wipe away the aboriginals in order to occupy the land and to exploit the resources. The whites have almost annihilated the Maoris of Australia and chased the rest from the main land. The Americans have brutally killed the Red Indians in order to occupy the land. These are the best examples of the attitude of the 'civilized' man against the so called 'uncivilized'. Here who is uncivilized? The inhuman white man is the uncivilized, and not the innocent aboriginal or tribal.

The tribals live by the forests. The resources of the forests are their means of survival. The forest is their habitat. Though forests are their habitat, they are chased away or evacuated in the name of development. The dominant classes also tried to deceive the tribals in order to acquire their land. They are economically, politically exploited, so also the tribal women are sexually exploited.

They are kept away from the main stream of the society. The cultural uprooting and the evacuation and the oppressions affect badly the life of the tribals. In every crime related to the forests, the mafia plays a vital role, but always the mafia, the police and the media accuse the tribals. They are the most alienated and oppressed group of people. They are also mistreated.

The triabls are ecologically conscious rivers and forests are their life. They protect the nature as nature provides for their daily survival. They have a strong feeling of oneness and community. They are willing to share the resources. It is to be kept in mind that the tribals are the people who are created by God in his image. They have their rights and dignity. They are not unequal or lesser human beings. In the Narmada valley project, 10 lakh tribals were evacuated from their habitat which was a grave injustice against them. It was a cruel act and was dehumanizing.

The tribals are tired of the oppressions so they are fighting for their autonomy. They struggle against the injustices to restore their land and rights. The Jarkhand is a supreme example for the assertion of autonomy. They would like to have their territorial integrity, their determination and government. In Wynad (Kerala), the tribals are struggling for their restoration of land. The society and the government have the responsibility to keep up the rights of the tribals. The church also has the responsibility to work for the liberation of the tribals as the agent of the Kingdom of God, which upholds the justice and rights.

Women

The patriarchy is a global phenomenon. Gender-discrimination is found in all cultures. They are being oppressed by the male chauvinistic society. They are idolized or objectified. Their dignity is questioned, rights are denied and their power to decide is curbed. The meaningful participation of women in the society is curtailed. Women were organizing themselves as a movement for their freedom. The dowry system, sexual violence, wife-beating and domestic violences are dehumanizing them.

The women movements and its ideology are influenced by several factors. Sociologically the victimization of women is the primary factor. The women's contributions are neglected. The projection is given to men and not to women. The fathers are referred and not the mothers. In India, in 33 minutes one woman is beaten by or undergoing cruelty of husband or their relatives. Dowry deaths are common in the Indian setting. Women are raped. The dalit women are asked to walk naked through the streets. Devadasi system, *sati* and child marriage are still found in India. It is reported that within 12 hours one bride is burned to death in India. Socially, economically and politically the women are powerless. Their condition in India is being improved, but still the atrocities against women are on the increase.

According to Tuttle, patriarchy is the 'universal political structure which privileges men at the expense of women'. The patriarchy is found in Jewish, Roman and Greek contexts. There was prejudice against women in Jewish context. The men pray, 'blessed art Thou O Lord of the universe, who has not made me a woman'. In Greek context Aristotle and Plato considered women as inferior beings. Demosthenes states, "women, we keep for the sake of pleasure, concubines for the ordinary requirements of the body, wives to bear children and to be faithful guardians of our household". Domestic situation was quite patriarchal. In the Indian context also women are objectified and their dignity and rights are not upheld.

The feminist ethics challenge the cultural aspects such as the use of language. The language is also patriarchal. The exclusive language which is silent about women. So it urged to have inclusive language (man-mankind, God as father-God as mother or parent, chairman-chairperson). The scriptures and liturgy are also male-dominated, so the feminists urges to change the exclusive language used. The traditional theology and the structure of the church are also not emphasizing the dignity and rights of women.

The women argue for the freedom. According to existential philosopher Martin Heidegger, voice of conscience is the basis of freedom. In the words of Jean-Paul-Sartre, man is condemned to be free. The meaning of existence is realized by exercizing the personal choice without any pressure from outside. The authentic existence for existentialism is the freedom of a person to decide for oneself. The women liberation movements challenges the authoritarian structure which curtails the freedom. The process that also helped the women's freedom, which affirms change and progress. We are free from the past to respond to the new possibility in the present context.

Feminism is focused on the injustice done to women in sexual, linguistic, social, economic, political, religious and ecclesiastical spheres. According to Katherine Doob Saken field the term feminist means as one who seeks justice and equality for all people and who is concerned for the fate of women. Judith Weidman indicates that feminist theology is not a theology solely about women, it has taken as the whole of humanity, and it touches on every contemporary issue. Elizabeth Schussler Fiorenza depicts feminist theology as critical theology is driven by the impetus to make the vision of Galatians 3:28 real within the Christian community.

There are five perspectives developed hermeneutically by feminists. There are mainly related to the interpretation of the Bible.

1. *Rejectionists*—They reject the text which deprive the freedom of women. Mary Daly was an example for this view. For them Christianity and Judaism are corrupt.
2. *Loyalists*—for them the fundamental principle of the essential validity and goodness of the Biblical tradition as word of God cannot be questioned.
3. *Revisionists*—They argue that the socio-cultural and historical milieu has made the tradition androcentric, but the text/tradition has the ability to reform itself. This model argues for the reform from within Bible. Phyllis Trible follows this view.
4. *Sublimationists*—They discuss the otherness of the feminine which is manifested in the form of feminine imagery and symbolism in human culture. It exalts the female traits higher than men.
5. *Liberationists*—They emphasis the liberation of the word from the clutches of patriarchal prejudices. It argues the struggle of the women to be liberated is the key hermeneutical position. Letty Russel and Fiorenza follow this model.

Feminism are of different kinds. Radical feminism is concerned of the ideology which would challenge the masculine prominence. Liberal feminism is concerned of the political rights of women. Socialist feminism is concerned of economic freedom and equality. Marxist feminism is arguing for the class struggle which aims at the dominance of the working class, including women. Recently, the Marxist feminism focuses attention on the gender discrimination/ exploitation. They argue for their meaningful participation. Eco-feminism looks at the impact of ecological crises and issues on women. The crises of ecology like of deforestation and scarcity of water are affecting the women (especially *dalit* and tribal women) than men.

In the book '*The church and second sex*', Mary Daly raises questions about sexism in the Catholic church. Daly charged that Catholicism was promoting a view of women that idealized and humiliated them. In reality the church was an enemy of sexual equality. For Daly, church is misogynist. In her view, the patriarchal psychologies also imprison women.

Elizabeth Schussler Fiorenza's main work is 'In memory of Her'. Her hermeneutics is influenced by Gadamer and Paul Ricoeur. In her view, hermeneutics is centred on the assumption that hermeneutics explores the dialogical interaction between the text and the contemporary interpreter in which the subject matter of the text comes into language. Biblical hermeneutics looks for understanding the text and its world as a rhetorical expression in a certain historical situation. She realizes the patriarchal ideology and androcentric spirit in the text. For her, feminist hermeneutics should aim at liberation of women. She argues for using historical and literacy critical methods in the interpretation.

The re-reading of the Bible from the context of the experience of the marginalized is widely accepted today. The women also re-read the Bible in doing a theology of liberation which would question the androcentrism and patriarchy found in all aspects of life and in Biblical and ecclesiastical tradition.

The feminist theology and ethics emerges out of the experience of the women. They undergo different suffering in the form of oppression. The patriarchal structures, cultural and systemic prejudice and violences and the socio-political and religious oppressions prevent freedom and the dignity of women. So they question the structures of oppression and aim at a praxis-oriented theology and ethics which is experiential, critical and liberative. It argues for the fairness or justice. The total transformation of the society in order to uphold justice is their vision. It is an ethics which ascertain the humanhood of women. It argues for their social, political and economic and ecclesiastical liberation.

The subaltern issues are very live today. Antonio Gramsci used the word to refer the working class or proletariat. They are the suffering ones in the world. They are the poor, oppressed and the marginalized. The subaltern groups are the alienated ones and are undergoing ill-treatment and discriminations. Their right to dignity and equality are denied. They are also dehumanized. They are recognized as the insignificant ones. They undergo the social and physical assault from the dominant. They are the victims of the patriarchy, the rich and the dominant class. The systemic violence is a threat to their dignified survival.

The righteous God is for the right of the subalterns. The poor and the marginated are the great concerns for God. As God is the creator, who made everyone in his image, he recognizes the dignity of the subalterns, though the dominant class reject their rights and dignity (Gen.1:27,28; LK. 4:16-21). God is for the restoration of the poor and the slaves (Lev.25). No one is supposed to neglect the aliens, landless, widows and the slaves (Ex 22; 20ff). God appears as the liberator of the subalterns. He identifies with the subalterns and have solidarity with them. The prophets were also quite firm on the issue of subalterns. They protested the capitalistic structure that did injustices against the subalterns (Am.2:6ff; 4:1ff; 5:10ff; Jere 5:23ff).

In the New Testament also the marginated are a significant group who had been oppressed by the evil structure of the time. The 'Nazareth Manifesto' challenges the oppression and it declares the freedom of the subalterns. 'Nazareth Manifesto' is the manifesto of the subalterns. Jesus' community was the community of the subalterns. The subaltern are understood as the blessed ones. The sick, the handicapped, the oppressed and the exploited ones are taken care by Jesus.

Jesus was radically challenging the evil and inhuman social system which curtailed the wellbeing of the people, especially the marginated. The feudal system which exploited the common people and made them more poor (Mt. 12:10ff; Mt.21:13ff). Jesus was the messiah of the subaltern and he was the trouble maker to the religious and political leaders of the time.

In the epistle of James also the concern for the subaltern is a significant issue. The 'faith and works' compact is for the liberation of the subaltern. James urges to give utmost care to the subaltern. In the community, the subaltern would be there, or they would be coming from outside to join the fellowship, but there should have real 'Kainonia' with them. Sharing of resources is to uplift the subaltern (Acts 2:43-47 and 4:32-35) so also the good works recommended by Apostle James is to uphold the subaltern (2:1-4; 2:14-20).

The liberative struggles are found essential for the emancipation of the subalterns. The exodus and the second exodus (Gen 12; Isa 40:1ff) portray the struggles of the subalterns. That movements of the subalterns were a political one. Bible has the vision of the society which is freed from unfair relationship and is based on the values of the Kingdom of God. Bible foresees and egalitarian society or a just community.

14

Modernism, Post-Modernism and Ethics

In ethics and theology changes are taking place because of the change of the context. There is a movement from colonialism to post-colonialism. The post-colonial situation is also neo-colonial. Now the colonialism is almost come to an end, but we see the fierce emergence of neo-colonialism, which is a new way of exploiting or oppressing the third world by the first world. Now we are also concerned of the movement from modernism to post-modernism. The present era is described as post-modern.

The modernism was a challenge to the traditional ethos. The enlightenment played a crucial role in the emergence of the modern. The importance given to human reason, scientific worldview and the humanism have contributed to modernism. The critical spirit and the freedom of thought and human potentiality are hailed in modernism. The development of science and technology placed man very high. The scientific rationality is developed so the people looked for the autonomy and freedom from religious and social structures. It is critical of what is authoritarian, superstitious and irrational.

The question of 'knowledge' is also very significant in the issue of modernism. 'I believe what can be observed' is positivism, which promotes experimentation in the understanding of knowledge. This view questioned the *a priori* knowledge and credibility of knowledge furnished by the church, traditional wisdom and dictated morality. The belief, the practices and the understanding of scriptures undergo radical changes. The empirical philosophy was a contribution of David Hume the Scottish philosopher who holds that knowledge is received though experience (matter—a fact experience) rather than religious experience. It is *a posteriori* and the speculative medieval theories of knowledge are absurd for them. The intellectual reasoning and the contextual experience are given utmost importance by them which is a significant contribution to modernism.

In post-modernism, there is chaoas—no authority or norm. The norms and authority are thrown off. The word post-modern is first appeared in the 1870, but it is widely used in the ensuing decades with different shades of meanings. According to Craig Bartholomew, the term post-modern in 1960s and 1980s emerged as a reaction to modernism in the arts. It is later found in the field of literature especially literary criticism. Ihab Hassan proposed the idea of a post modern literature of silence which is anti-representationalist and anti-modernist in its move towards disorder and attack on form (Themelios, January 1975, p. 25). The indeterminancy (not fixed, vague) also contributed to post modernity. It is explained that indeterminancy relates to heterodoxy, pluralism, ecclecticism, randomness revolt and deformation. Imminence and indeterminancy are understood as the heart of post-modern episteme (*Ibid*., p. 26). The philosophical (ideas, culture, arts, religion) and social (capitalism, politics, communications) shifts are all ingredients in post-modern (*Ibid*., p. 26).

David Lyon sums up the modernity as follows, "modernity is all about the massive changes that took place at many levels from the mid-sixteenth century onwards, changes signalled by the shifts that uprooted agricultural workers and transformed them into mobile industrial urbanites. Modernity questions all conventional ways of doing things, substituting authorities of its own, based in science, economic growth, democracy or law. And it unsettles the self, if identity is given in traditional society, in modernity it is constructed" (quoted by Craig Bartholomew, *Ibid*., p. 27). The meaninglessness and aloneness (the society of strangers) and ecological crises becomes the order of the day, which contribute to crisis in modernism, and its name is post-modernity. According to Brian D. Ingraffia, "whereas modernism tried to elevate man into God's place, post-modern theory seeks to destroy or deconstruct the very place and attributes to God" (*Post-modern Theory and Biblical Theology: Vanquishing God's Shadow,* p.1). In post-modernism man is only a tiny being among the realities. Nietschzes transvaluation of values and elimination of God ('God is dead') have influenced the post modernity.

Jurgen Habermas challenged the view that post-modernity is the end of modernity. For him modernity is an unfinished project. In the view of Jean-Francois Lyotard, post-modern condition is characterized by incredulity (unwilling to believe) towards metanarratives. Metanarratives are those large narratives that undergirded and legitimized the knowledge enterprise in modernity. It is said that the legitimation of knowledge always requires some narrative, but, in the post-modern context, such narratives are incredible. The grand narratives have lost its validity. The post-modernity challenged the possibility of the transcendent, and the validity of the narratives are made local. There is no consensus, in Lyotard's view on true knowledge (Themalios January, 1997, p. 28).

Jacques Derrida is famous for his attempts on deconstruction. He tries to dismantle the Judaeo-Christian roots of metaphysics by his deconstruction. In his deconstruction of onto theology he considers that Christian theology as a prime example of logocentric metaphysics. He also feels that Christian theology is unable to guard against foreign philosophical influences (Brian D. Ingraffia, *Post-modern Theory and Biblical Theology*, p.13).

According to Craig Bartholomew, as Thiselton points out, deconstruction in literary theory is often perceived as the strongest philosophical context of post-modernism and Derrida is one of the exponent (*Ibid.*, p. 29). For Derrida, language is the bottom line of reality and it is unable to represent the reality accurately. In his view there is also textual instability. For him, writing is prior to speech, writing is not mere inscription. Writing is related to every system of communication—pictorial, musical and sculptural writing (*Ibid.*, p. 30).

Fragmentation and transience characterise post-modernity accompanied by thorough going pluralism, says Craig Bartholomew (*Ibid.*, p. 30). Derrida does not see any firm grounding of language which is nit illusory. In Craig Bertholomew's, post-modernity has raised all sorts of questions about our capacity to know and how we know and whether we can accurately to represent reality, i.e, about epistemology. The possibility of universal knowledge is considered as impossible and it considers all knowledge to be local, communal and human construct. It undermined the rationality, autonomous view of human which was dominant in modernity. In his view, post-modernity is characterized by pluralism, uncertainty, instability and fragmentation. The old certainties seem to have gone, with no unified vision to replace them (*Ibid.*, p. 32). Post modernity leads to relativism.

In modernity, the factors like secularization, urbanization and the science and technology have contributed positively and negatively the society. In the ethical reflection also these factors made greater impacts. There was a wise and responsible use of science (knowledge) and also the abuse of science and technology. Man's potentiality and knowledge went even to the extreme to ruthlessly tap the resource and spoilt the atmosphere by their industrial enterprise and brought the ecological crisis which became a severe threat to survival. At the same time, the irrationality and superstitions were questioned and humanness was upheld. The traditional value system and religious authority come under the attack. A new awareness of the reality was emerged which questioned the discriminations and argued for freedom. Modernism was a boon and a bane. If the responsibility is lost, any system or ideology can be curse. Evaluating the crisis of modernism Dr. K.C. Abraham has said that it is hazardous to life as it is destroying the basic fabric of human relationships.

The neo-colonial forces played a very crucial role to control the economic structure as they appeared in the form of IMF, MNCs and TNCs. It was also a bad effect of modernism. Modernism paved the way for different kinds of developments which were misused by the capitalistic forces. The impact of post-modernity is a very crucial issue to discuss with. In globalization the post-modernity has an impact. Globalization is a free market consumerist ideology where the persons are not important, but the products and money. Man is only a spectator and he is a tiny being among several things around. The pluralism that supports the different experiences and realities and so also the relativism which contribute to ethical pluralism.

The relativism is related to fragmentation and uncertainty which the post-modernism promotes. Homogenization and universalization are being challenged. The ethical norms also undergo radical threat. Ethics will be relativistic or ethics becomes absurd. There is no set standards as everything is uncertain or vague. It nihiliates God so also the ethical norms and value systems. There can be misuse of freedom or absolute freedom where nobody is mutually responsible. Post-modernism provides a new culture, a new social structure, a new worldview and a new 'morality' as against the existing and traditional. It is after the new trends in all aspects of life.

15

Ethics for a New World: Towards an Evaluative Approach

One of the dilemma of man is that he does always undergo the crisis situation. There are normative principles to guide a person to get rid of the pitfalls. The laws are given to instruct the people. The Decalogue is one of the best examples for the normative rules given. They can be called as the norms or the *a priori* rules. They are quite important for the functioning of the society. The rules or regulations are given as guide of conduct to steer the society. One of the problem with the rule is the double standards set by people. There are 'Rules and rules'. There are rules to be applied to the common people and 'Rules' that are applied to the dominant. The dominants are always above the rules.

The laws can be reduced to be inhuman and legalistic. The rigidity of the law is dangerous and it does not serve the love. The law is supposed to the humane, but it is so happened that the rigidity of the law suppress the Spirit of the law. In Indian context also as in most of the other contexts legalism is very much found in the law. The context is not regarded much. 'Rules for rules' sake are applied disregarding the situation and also the merit of the case. The religious traditions base their ethics and theology on the *a priori* rules. They hold on a normative approach. The ethical codes are important to curb the persons from committing mistakes.

Even when we uphold the normative principles, it is significant to evaluate the issues from the Christian principle of love, mercy and generosity. In the context of the victimized it is not fitting to apply the normative. The normative rules cannot help the person or persons in the crisis. The legalistic attitude should be examined as the *a priori* rules are not helpful to guide the persons in the crisis. Those who violated the normative principles are in crisis and they should be under girded. Do we have the responsibility to help those who commited adultery, divorce, murder, abortion and stealing? One of the crucial thing is to analyse the context of the person who is in the crisis. There might be psycho-social factors behind certain problems. The cultural, social, psychological and genetic factors that influence some issues. 'Stealing' can be the influence of social, cultural and genetic factors. Polyandry and polygamy are the cultural patterns of certain communities. These are very common amongst the tribal communities, as they are accepted practices of the society.

The legitimation of evil should not be appreciated. The evil has to be strongly challenged, and it should not be legitimized. No one is supposed to continue in evil. Those who are the victims of the situation are to be helped by making a fitting response. *A priori* or normative rules are suiting to guide or instruct persons and communities to get away from the mistakes or evil. They are a great help in the form of commandments. But those who violated the rules or what is normative and is facing the dilemma should not be considered in the light of the normative. Those who are in crisis and seeking mercy are to be taken into account from the evaluative approach. The evaluative approach can be also called *a posteriori-agapeic* approach. This can be applied to those who violated the normative rules. Here also the role of sin and the conversion (repentence) are to be considered seriously. Love always grant mercy to the repentant, though he/she violated the normative. The evaluative approach is to show love and mercy to those who undergo the crisis situations which can be termed as posterior (that which comes after).

Jesus was affirming the importance of what is normative, but at the same time he was applying the evaluative approach to support, guide and restore those who are in crisis. Jesus condemned the evil and he gave utmost importance to the command and the normative principles. But at the same time, he was conscious of the psycho-social factors that influence a person and responding responsibly in the situation. When Jesus was dealing the Samaritan woman and also the woman caught in adultery (John chapters 4 and 8), he was using the evaluative approach (*a posteriori*-agapeic approach) so that they could be helped in that situation. Helping the persons in the crisis will curb the further evil. In the above stated cases, they were redeemed from the situation, but commanded them 'sin no more'. This clearly shows that Jesus was never legitimizing evil. He was forgiving the sinner, but condemning the sin. Jesus' evaluative perspective towards adultery is not legitimizing the immoral act, but evaluated the context and derive at conclusion on the merit of each case. While Jesus applied the evaluative approach, he was conscious of the deliberate violation of norms and manipulations of the dominant such as Pharisees and condemned them.

Apostle Paul was also conscious of the need of an evaluative approach. He did give importance to the normative but he was quite flexible in the cases of the victimized. The persons who committed incest is restored as he was repenting about it. He was not a legalist to apply normative principle in that crisis situation. But he was applying the *a posteriori* agapeic approach to save the person from bad to worse.

In the context of the crisis of persons and the communities, the Christian principles such as love, mercy and generosity are playing very crucial roles to understand and to deal with them in a spirit of amity and harmony. When the individuals or communities become the objects of mercy, care and love, the Christian responsibility is to understand and to render help to the people in their crises. What is absent in Indian context is a evaluative perspective which can cater to the need. The ethical need is to suggest or propose and evaluative approach which would analyse and understand the situation and to treat the cases with charity and generosity, which would help to maintain and foster love, peace, care, humanness and harmony among communities. The evaluative approach can be applied to the global context also.

The evaluative approach could analyse the situation to realize the need of the persons in the context and to help the persons or communities in their moral dilemmas. It is important to evaluate the situation of a persons rather than applying the normative principles disregarding the context. The evaluative perspective is to interpret the situation to know what decision would bring good to the persons. It is a loving and restoring principle to persons and human communities in moral crisis. Evaluative perspective will help to interpret the situations and to assess the would-be consequences so that evil effect could be reduced and greater goodwill be realized in the issues. It enables to avoid what is bad and inhuman.

What is needed to the moral crises in the Indian context is to propose an ethical approach which can help christians to relate meaningfully with other communities. It is important to have an approach to held those who are in crisis. The norm of ethics is *a priori* rules and principles. This is found in all religious traditions. The normative principles are important, but what is required an evaluative approach in the context of our times. This would help to enhance love, mercy, generosity, peace, and harmony.

The reckless condemnation of any practice or any issue in the context is not the answer to the problem. An evaluative ethical approach which is agapeic and contextual has to be suggested because it can only help the people to deal the issues with care and concern. It is to be noted that socio-economic, psychological and historical factors also have contributed to the crises of the individuals and communities. The individuals and communities are seeking sympathy, compassion, love, and mercy. They look for help and it is the christian obligation to offer help in the crises of the people.

Showing generosity or mercy for the good is to be affirmed. In the cases (the experience or what is posterior), the individuals or communities are at our mercy. The Christian responsibility is not to condemn those who are the victims of mistakes or crises, but to consider their welfare and good as part of Christian love or charity. Here one can find the relevance or adequacy of *a posteriori-agapeic* approach. The norm is certainly the apriori rules or principles. The *a posteriori-agapeic* approach is not suggested as the normative principle, but only as an evaluative approach.

Conclusion

The 'Christian ethics': issues and insight is not only giving an orientation, but also helping us to have an in-depth look at the various issues. It will enable us to re-orient our lives according to God's will. The awareness to the reality around (context) and the Biblical vision is important to have a proper understanding of our responsibility. The significance of the evaluative approach is considered in this book which can be an eye opener to the rigid and legalistic ethical methodologies which curtail the freedom, love and humanness.

The adequate ethical approach should have a dialectics of the reflections on the context and the Bible as the Bible is given in a context. It is to respond to the live issues of humanity in the present context. The contextual dimension and the role of love are to be given utmost importance in Christian Ethics.

Bibliography

Barrett, C.K., *The Gospel According to John*, London: S.P.C.K., 1962.

Beach, Waldo and Richard Niebuhr Ed. *Christian Ethics: Sources of Living tradition*, 2nd edn, (New York : Alfred A. Knopf, 1973).

Bornkamm, Gunther, *Jesus of Nazareth*, trans. Irene and Fraser McLuskey with James M. Robinson (fifth impression), London: Hodder & Stoughton, 1979.

Bonino, Jose Miguez. *Toward a Christian political ethics*, London: SCM Press Ltd., 1983.

Bonino, Jose Miguez. *Room to be people*, Geneva: W.C.C. 1975

Bultmann, Rudolf, *Theology of the New Testament,* Vol.1, London: S.C.M. Press Ltd., 1974.

Bultmann, Rudolf, *The Gospel of John : A Commentary*, trans. G.R. Beasley-Murray, edited by R.U.N. Hoare and J.K. Riches, Philadelphia: The Westminster Press, 1971.

Bultmann, Rudolf, *Jesus and the Word,* London: Collins, 1958.

Carl F. Henry, *Bakers Dictionary of Christian Ethics* (U.S.A. : Baker Book House, 1973).

Cox, Harvey, *The situation ethics debate,* Philadelphia: Westminster Press, 1968.

Composta, *Doria, Moral Philosophy and Social Ethics,* Bangalore : Theological Publications in India, 1988).

Conzelmann, *Hans, Jesus* (Reprint), Philadelphia: Fortress Press, 1975.

Curran, Charles E. *Ongoing Revision in Moral Theology,* Notra Dome. Fides Publishers, 1975.

Curran, Charles E. *A new look at Christian Morality*, London: Shed and Ward, 1976.

Dodd, C.H., *Gospel and the Law*, Cambridge: University Press, 1957.

Dodd, C.H., *The Interpretation of the Fourth Gospel*, Cambridge; University Press, 1968.

Dunn, James D.G., *Unity and Diversity in the New Testament*, London: S.C.M. Press Ltd., 1981.

Dunn, James D.G., *Jesus Paul and the Law: Studies in Mark and Galatians*, Kentucky: Westminster/John Knox Press, 1990.

Edanad, Antony, *Christian Experience and the New Covenant*, Bangalore: Dharmaram Publications, 1987.

Erickson, Millard J., "Fletcher Joseph" In *Baker's Dictionary of Christian* edited by Carl.F. Henry (U.S.A.: Bakers Book House, 1973).

Fletcher, Joseph, *Moral Responsibility: Situation Ethics at Work*, Philadelphia: Westminster Press, 1967.

Fletcher, Joseph. "Ethical Aspects of Genetic Control" in *Bio-Ethics* edited by Thomas A. Shannon (New York : Paulist Press, 1976).

Fletcher, Joseph. "Indicators of Humanhood: A Tentative Profile of Man" *In Bio-Ethics* edited by Thomas A. Shannon (New York: Paulist Press, 1970).

Fletcher, Joseph, ed. *Christianity and Property*. (Philadelphia: The Westminster Press, 1977).

Frankena, William K. *Ethics* (New Delhi : Prentice-Hall of India, 1988).

Gill, Robin, *A Textbook of Christian Ethics* (Edinburg: T. & T. Chark Ltd., 1985).

Giesler, Norman. *Options in Contemporary Christian Ethics* (Michigan : Baker Book House, 1991).

Gregories, Paulose Mar. *Science for Sane Societies* (Madras : C.L.S., 1980).

Hazelton, Roser. "Humanism and Hmanitarianism" In *Dictionary of Christian Ethics* edited by John Macquerre, London : SCM Ltd., 1967)

Harrington, Daniel J., *John's thought and theology: An Introduction*, Good news Series Vol. 33, Wilmington: Michael Glazier Inc., 1990

Hendriksen, William, *The Gospel of John,* Pennsylvania: The Banner of Truth Trust, 1976.

Heth, William A. and Gordon J. Wenham, *Jesus and Divorce: The Problem with Evangelical Consensus*, Nashville: Thomas Nelson Publishers, 1984.

Houlden, J.L., *Ethics of the New Testament*, New York: Oxford University Press Ltd., 1971.

Kadankavil, Thomas. *Ethical world*, Bangalore: Dharmaram publications, 1995.

Kuhn, Harold. B. "Relativism" In Baker's *Dictionary of Christian Ethics* edited by Carl F. Henry (Michigan: Baker Book House, 1981).

Ladd, George Eldon, *A Theology of the New Testament*, Michigan: William B. Eerdman's Publishing Company, 1974.

Lammers, Stephen E. and Allen Verkey, ed. *On Moral Medicine* (Michigan : William B. Eerdmans Publsihing Co., 1987).

Lane, William L., *The Gospel According to Mark*, Michigan: William B. Eerdman's Publishing Company, 1975.

Lange, Nicholas, De, *Judaism,* Oxford: University Press, 1986. Martin, R.P., "Judaism" *In the New Bible Dictionary* (reprint), edited by J.D. Douglas, England: Inter Varsity Press, 1976.

Lillie, William. *An introduction to Ethics*. New Delhi Allied Publishers Ltd., 1989.

Lobo, George V. *Current Problems in Medical Ethics*. Allahabad: St. Paul Publications, 1980.

Lutzer, Edwin. *The Necessity of Ethical Absolutes.* Michigan: Zonderavan Publishing House, 1981.

Luke, K., "Society Divided by Religion: The Jewish World of Jesus' Time" *In Bible Bhasyam* Vol. 1, No.3 (September 1975), pp.195-209.

Lehmann, Paul L. *Ethics in a Christian context,* New York: Harper and Row Publishers, 1963.

Mabry, Hunter P. ed. *Christian ethics-An Introductory Reader,* Serampore: Senate of Serampore College, 1987.

Michalson, Carl. "Existentialist Ethics" *in Dictionary of Christian Ethics* edited by John Macquarrie London: SCM Ltd., 1967.

Mitchell, Basil, "Ideals, Roles and Rules" *Norm and Contest in Christian Ethics.* Gene H. Outka and Paul Ramsey. London : SCM Press, 1968.

Moltmann, Jurgen. *Theology of Hope, New York:* Harper and Row, 1967.

Niebuhr, Richard H. *The Responsible self: An essay in Christian Moral philosophy,* New York: Harper and Row publishers, 1963.

Pannenberg, Wolfhart. *Theology and the Kingdom of God,* Philadelphia: Westminster press, 1969.

Pathrapankal, Joseph, *Christian Life: New Testament Perspectives,* Bangalore: Dharmaram Publications, 1982.

Prabhu, George M. Soares, "The Dharma of Jesus: An Interpretation of the Sermon on the Mount" *In Bible Bhashyam,* Vol. VI, No.4 (December 1980), pp.358-81

Pudussery, Paul S., "Jesus' Teaching on family life" *In Bible Bhashyam,* Vol. XVII, No. 4 (December 1991), pp. 217-41.

Peschke, Karl. H. *Christian Ethics,* Vol. 1. Bangalore : TPI, 1987.

Peschke, Karl. H. *Christian Ethics,* Vol. II. Bangalore: TPI, 1987.

Quinton, Anthony. *Utilitarian Ethics.* London : Macmillan Press, 1973.

Robinson, J.A.T. *Christian Morals Today,* Philadelphia : Westminster press, 1964.

Ramsey, Paul. *The Basic Christian Ethics,* Chicago The University of Chicago Press, 1980.

Rauschenbush, Walter. *A Theology for the Social Gospel,* New York: Macmillan, 1918.

Ramsey, Paul. "Justice and Equal Treatment" *On Moral Medicine* edited by Stephen E. Lammers and Allen Verkey, Michigan: William B. Eerchmans Publishing Co., 1987.

Ramsey, Paul, "A Christian approach to the question of Sexual relations outside marriage", *Journal of Religion,* Vol. XLV, No.2 (April, 1968), pp. 202-12.

Sykes, Marjorie. *Quakers in India.* London : George Allen & Unwin, 1980.

Sanders, E.P., *Jesus and Judaism,* London: S.C.M. Press Ltd., 1985.

Schnackenburg, Rudolf, *The Moral Teachings of the New Testament,* Kant: Burns & Oates, 1982.

Schweitzer, Edward, *The Gospel According to Mark,* London S.P.C.K., 1978.

Schweitzer, Edward, *The Goodnews According to Mathew,* Atlanta: John knox Press, 1975.

Scott, Ernst F., *The Ethical Teaching of Jesus,* New York: The Macmillan Co., 1925.

Stott, John R.W., *Christian Counter-culture: The Message of the Sermon on the Mount* (Reprint), England: Inter-Versity Press, 1978.

Srampical, Thomas. "Artificial Insemination and Invitrofertilization", *Jeevadhara*, Vol. XXII, No. 132 (Novermber 1992), pp. 468-83.

Tillich, Paul. My Search for Absolutes. New York : Simon & Schuster, 1967.

Vadackumcherry, Joseph. *Natural-law-Morality Versus Situationism in Morals*. Cochin : Louis Memorial Press, 1969.

Vellanickal, Mathew, *Studies in the Gospel of John,* Bangalore : Asian Trading Corporation, 1982.

Von Hildebrand, Alice and Dietrich. *Morality and Situation Ethics* Chicago : Fransiscan Herald Press, 1966.

White, R.E.O., *Biblical Ethics: The Changing Continuity of Christian Ethics,* Vol. 1, Exeter: The Paternoster Press, 1979.

INDEX